MW00583265

PRAISE FOR BRIAN CLAYPOOL

Brian Claypool is a gifted advocate and storyteller both inside and outside the courtroom, with a commanding presence. His deep connection with and commitment to his clients manifests in his words and in his eyes. Understanding his complex life story and his journey will reveal the genesis of his passion for justice for children who have been hurt by those whom they trusted. This has led to great success for the causes of his clients.

—Retired Judge Gail A. Andler
Orange County, California Superior Court

BREAK
THE
CODE
OF
SILENCE

BREAK THE CODE OF SILENCE

RAISING MY VOICE TO PROTECT OUR KIDS

BRIAN CLAYPOOL

FLASH POINT

Published by Flashpoint™ Books, Seattle
www.flashpointbooks.com

Produced by Girl Friday Productions

Author photo © Cierra Porter
Photo page xx courtesy of the author

Cover design: David Fassett
Production editorial: Laura Dailey
Project management: Dave Valencia

ISBN (hardcover): 978-1-954854-74-1
ISBN (ebook): 978-1-954854-76-5

Library of Congress Control Number: 2022920169

First edition

CONTENTS

PART IV—BREAKING THE CODE OF SILENCE:
WARNING SIGNS OF CHILD ABUSE

AUTHOR'S NOTE

No part of this book or my observations are intended to be a substitute for legal advice or recommendations in any context from a lawyer/legal counsel. The reader should consult a lawyer in all legal matters, particularly regarding children or anything that may require legal advice.

The story I share is factual and true. Some of the descriptions are graphic in nature and may be difficult to read or may be unsuitable for minors.

FOREWORD

History has a way of wedging itself into the fabric of your life at the most beautiful and inopportune times, both of which can occur without warning. In *Break the Code of Silence*, Brian Claypool takes us on a journey through his life. He shares the damage from his childhood trauma and the code of silence he lived by until now. As a result of that silence, Brian internalized fear, pain, loss, anxiety, and lack of confidence. No one advocated on behalf of Brian, because some didn't know what was occurring and others failed to question his circumstances or their observations.

Adults may assume that children will have a lifetime to forget or recover from painful experiences due to childhood abuse. However, many can recall the most insignificant details and simply "unpleasant" occurrences. Our minds are vast and our bodies are memory storage systems. The pain is still there.

The Las Vegas massacre was a tragic event that took lives and traumatized people. Amid chaos and fear, it created new trauma and triggered recollections from Brian's childhood—memories that he had long ago buried.

Brian courageously shares his story to show the damage

done to children who are victims of sexual, emotional, physical, and mental abuse. Brian does not compare his childhood to those of the victims he has represented; *Break the Code of Silence* informs us of the damage childhood trauma causes and how it can impede progress and decrease confidence, faith, and trust, forcing people onto paths they never intended to travel. We cannot discount others' experiences or trauma based on our judgment of their severity. It is not always about the severity; it's about how others process and internalize their trauma and their beliefs regarding the world around them, and how these beliefs influence behaviors. For example, twin brothers who grew up in the same household can have different desires, goals, beliefs, interests, and lifestyles—not strictly due to experiences, but how they are processed.

When we hear stories in the media about sexually abused children—it happens so often—they're treated as though the trauma will dissipate with time. "What goes on in this house stays in this house" maintains that code of silence and further perpetuates the damage. If a child cannot go to a parent for safety—then who? How do they learn to trust adults, and how does an adult learn to trust others to help? Brian shines a light on these issues and offers solutions to every one of them.

Therapists often treat the types of individuals that Brian has represented, and many of their stories have not made it to daylight. Brian's endeavors to learn from his trauma allowed him to discover it was preventable. He utilizes his skill set to protect and provide justice for children, invisible to society, who were violated in the worst ways possible—until society is forced to acknowledge their suffering.

Everyone who works with children—parents, teachers, mentors, social workers—needs to pay attention to the red flags that Brian shares. The warnings are not difficult to spot. We simply must tune in and care more about children—all people—and speak up to prevent what is preventable. It's better to question what does not appear normal and be wrong than to be silent and allow the cycle to continue.

Brian has made it his mission—his life's work—to protect the innocent and encourage breaking the code of silence. Children are innocent until they are forced onto another path that they did not choose, which then affects their adulthood.

In reading *Break the Code of Silence*, please pay attention to the indicators but also to your intuition, which may seem insignificant at that moment, because speaking out can make a difference. The red flags Brian shares are warnings that if missed or ignored can cost children their lives or affect their mental health. Recognizing these flags can help you with your children, or children in general, as we are all responsible for protecting them.

Red flags are warnings, *not consequences*; they help you catch abuse sooner, so you can prevent it from happening rather than look at the consequences after it has already occurred. Brian's emotional response to the Las Vegas massacre was a result of those red flags being disregarded during his childhood.

Red flags are often identified and highlighted in therapy sessions or courtrooms by experts—but why allow it to get to that point? If unaddressed, these red flags are also indicators of future behaviors. Childhood experiences—good and bad—influence development. They can manifest in several ways from small to extremely impactful. Some children may end up disconnected from family and friends, while others have a diminished range of emotions.

We must become mindful of our behaviors and communication toward children, create nurturing environments for them, have healthy boundaries, and agree to encourage children to speak out when something does not feel right. If their concerns or situations are addressed respectfully and with care and urgency, we can teach them to *trust* us and tell us when they feel uncomfortable or have been threatened or harmed. Trust can begin to facilitate breaking the code of silence.

Alyssa Curry, MA, LPC

INTRODUCTION

Just as I don't know the full story of anyone else's life, they don't know mine. And to an extent, there's only so much we're aware of about our own lives. There are always pieces that are intentionally or subconsciously buried. Sometimes they're simply forgotten or repressed, yet still, the choices we make—the way we live and the things we do—are because of them.

I thought time would remove the dust-covered remnants of the trauma I experienced as a child. Years later, as though it were my predetermined course, I realized that time intentionally linked me to more. The way I ultimately responded to the abuse and dysfunction of my childhood contributed to who I have become—a servant of God, a loving father, and a determined litigation and civil rights lawyer. Yet for countless others, trauma and dysfunction obliterate an intended path, forcing them onto another. Although my experiences threatened to derail me, I found a saving grace—*my faith*. My relationship with God has helped me to recognize that my journey is not about forgetting or ignoring my experiences, but about letting them transform me. It is about using my intimate understanding of abuse to inform and fuel my efforts to help others.

For years, I've been consumed with fighting vile sexual abuse, molestation, discrimination, and civil rights violations. Working in the trenches is uncomfortable and not a place that others *want* to go, but the *need* is there. The trenches are morally impure, dirty, filled with buried secrets and monstrous, unimaginable crimes. I'm fighting—always fighting and asking direct questions to uncover excuses, lies, manipulation—the entire reprehensible gamut.

Why fight for someone who doesn't know or even believe they have a voice? There are myriad reasons. If we help them find their voice and share their truth, together, these voices can tell a story. It's not one we want to hear, but if we are to stop ongoing abuse and prevent future trespasses, we must. Opening ourselves to the reality of abuse is never easy, but illuminating these types of crimes is the right thing to do. When we are forced to see, we are forced to care, to find solutions, and to change laws.

Talking about abuse never gets easier. I still find it revolting to handle cases where voices were intentionally silenced. When dealing with trauma and empathizing with the pain and suffering my clients have endured, regardless of the outcome of the case, it's impossible to walk away unchanged. If you care about humanity, about children, and about the truth, any trespass against them alters you.

Though exhausting, it is my emotional attachment to each case that fuels me. The horror these children and their families suffered becomes engrained in my mind as a reminder that hidden in plain sight are countless more children who are ready to tell their story. They need help, healing, and retribution. As for those who can't speak out because they perished as a result of abuse, they need justice. The perpetrators must be held accountable for the consequences of their despicable acts. These children, and their parents, deserve help in fighting to defend their young lives against predators and the people who protect them and who attempt to subvert justice. Those who have been abused, along with their loved ones, need to know they matter and are heard.

As the largest child abuse case at a single school in the history of this country, the Miramonte sexual abuse case was an emotional, nearly four-year battle that garnered significant attention and became a landmark case. The atrocities that took place were utterly disturbing, making it especially unfathomable that anyone would protect the pedophiles who had abused and molested these children. In the first wave of settlements, sixty-five victims settled out of court for, on average, $400,000 before litigation began. The Claypool Law Firm, a boutique litigation firm, represented nineteen children in the second wave, who, together with sixty-two clients represented by three other law firms, settled for an average of a little under $2 million per child.

Before Miramonte, my law firm represented six African American children who were literally tortured by their foster parents. Instead of owning up to their considerable failings, those administering the child care system, which should have protected these children and didn't, fought back. They attempted to foist the responsibility of child advocacy onto someone else. In reality, heinous crimes were committed on their watch, and they had the information and resources to stop them, but they didn't. You will read about these two cases later in this book, but they serve as glaring examples of why we need to uncover even the most sordid details of abuse and attempts to cover it up, and to prosecute such cases to the fullest extent of the law.

In my extensive experience, red flags are nearly always evident when there is abuse, especially sexual abuse. Sexual abuse against children does not happen overnight. Typically, it is an extended process that includes grooming the victims. There's a saying that when something's not right, it's wrong. All too often, even the brightest and biggest red flags are repeatedly ignored. In both of the cases I just mentioned, numerous people were aware that something was wrong, but said or did nothing to investigate or, once the abuse was apparent, stop it. In this book, I will share common red flags in the hopes that should you encounter them, you will see them for the warning signs they are and feel empowered to speak up.

But why do we ignore red flags in the first place? To me, this behavior, this attitude of ignorance, points to a more widespread societal issue—a destructive *code of silence* under which crimes like these and many others are allowed to persist. Adults are uncomfortable speaking up. They may be afraid of leveling a false accusation, or getting someone in trouble, or getting in trouble themselves for not having spoken up earlier. But what about the children who are being abused? Why aren't we at least as afraid of not protecting those who are incapable of protecting themselves? The code of silence grants perpetrators the time to claim additional victims and destroy more lives. Children are already vulnerable, and underserved youth and immigrants are even easier targets for predators, who know our system doesn't have the same value or concern for those on the margins.

Throughout parts II and III of this book, I highlight some of the red flags that were present as I was growing up and in some of the landmark court cases in which I've represented victims of abuse. Once we learn to look for red flags and see them as what they are—warning signs that abuse is, or may be, occurring—it will help us break the code of silence.

When it comes to children, power and credibility are perilously unbalanced. We are more concerned with protecting the powerful than the vulnerable. In the cases I've worked and won, the systems, organizations, and individuals responsible for protecting children deliberately concealed the truth when they could have prevented these perpetrators from extending their reach. Once you know, you are unquestionably accountable.

In each case, I have had to uncover how and why organizations and individuals who are in place to protect children *don't*, and consistently, the common denominator is the code of silence. The question is what's in it for them, because clearly they have an agenda. Typically, it's money. Preserving their public image and ensuring a lifeline of revenue too often trumps child safety. And that's one of the reasons it's essential to levy significant financial penalties on these institutions—to show that if the primary concern is money, they will face far greater losses when they adhere to the code of silence than when they speak up and take action.

After more than twenty-five years in law, I contemplated slowing down and doing other things that would assist our youth and benefit society. One of these was starting a nonprofit organization to help children transition out of foster care when they turn eighteen. Experience has taught me there are aspects of life that children in foster care may not be prepared for, and I thought that if I helped with their transition, it might make their move into adulthood a bit smoother.

First, however, I decided to take the time to clear my head and to think through my past decisions and my personal journey. Sharing my story is a part of that journey.

PART I

THE LAS VEGAS MASSACRE

1

In my life, I've had a handful of select good friends. In social environments, I've been extremely outgoing. That is, until that fateful day, when my life changed forever. I will never forget the sights and sounds of that day, nor the panic and terror I felt. Those images and sensations are burned into my brain and seared into my soul. But it had a compound effect as well, causing earlier life trauma to boil to the surface and damage me even further.

This book isn't about me—not really. But I'm starting with my own story because, often, people can relate better when they know where you're coming from or where you've been. Once you see where I've been, you'll understand why it is that I do what I do, and why my work of advocating for victims of trauma and violence means so much to me.

For a long time now, I've spent much of my time alone. As a kid, that was circumstantial—it was just the way life was. Today, it's by preference. If I'm not jogging, walking, working, or with my beautiful daughter, Alana, who is now seventeen, I prefer my own company. Perhaps it's how I detox from life.

So it wasn't unusual that I'd purchased a single VIP pass

to the Route 91 Harvest Festival in Las Vegas. As I'd done on many other occasions, I planned to enjoy the three-day music festival on my own to celebrate my birthday. Eric Church, Jake Owen, Jason Aldean, Maren Morris, and several others were performing. The concert was scheduled to begin on Friday, ending with Jason Aldean on Sunday evening, October 1, 2017. It was unusual for me to take a break from work for an entire weekend, but at the time, I had a lot to consider. I'd been thinking about decreasing my workload at my law firm, but I wasn't sure. Perhaps a little time away would help me gain some perspective. My tentative plans were to fly out on Saturday morning, catch the concert that evening, and return home to Pasadena on Sunday morning.

On the morning of September 30, I checked into Mandalay Bay and rode the elevator to the twenty-sixth floor. I entered the room and took in the incredible panoramic view of the makeshift concert area below. I could see everything. The concert area was across the street in a big, open lot partially enclosed by a fence. There were two stages. Both had tons of stage lighting, aluminum bleachers, and a plethora of concession stands. A handful of towering palm trees bordered the area. The remainder of the space was left open, and I envisioned it would serve as standing room or lawn seating for thousands. Anticipating a great concert, I shifted into the mindset of relaxing and enjoying the day. I changed into a pair of shorts and went to lounge by the pool until 4:00 that afternoon, when it was time to head over to the venue.

The concert began at 7:30 that evening, and as expected, Maren Morris did not disappoint. Sam Hunt followed with a solid performance, and I did my share of toe tapping and clapping with the rest of the audience. People were dancing as carefree as I'd seen in a long time. Everyone around me seemed happy, free of worry, and in the moment. I was, too. Other than time with my daughter, my days didn't generally include much fun or relaxation. More often, I was working closely with clients, identifying with their pain and suffering and trying to get retribution for what they'd been through. I was working to advocate for them and to create the kind of meaningful change that would protect others from experiencing what my clients had experienced. After the cases I'd been working, it was time to take a break and regroup for the next round. There would always be more.

The music festival delivered a welcome, if temporary, reprieve. The fresh air, coupled with uplifting country music, was what my soul needed. Hearing people of all ages singing as loud as they could, whether they knew the right words or not, was entertaining. I even found myself belting out a few bars to Maren's songs. It was fun. I hadn't let my guard down in quite a while because I was always fighting for someone.

I left the concert in a good place that evening, trailing a casual, yet steady, flow of concertgoers across the bridge toward Mandalay Bay. I slipped inside, eyeing a comfortable bar area where I decided to grab a seat and have a nightcap. All around me, the atmosphere was overflowing with excitement from the concert. Sound effects from slot machines, background music, and people gambling at tables amplified the festive energy. I sat next to a group of women and found that they, too, were from Southern California. They chatted about Vegas, the concert, and their favorite songs, making it apparent they were real fans of several artists. There were so many friendly people at the festival, it made me feel like I hadn't gone alone. All it seemed any of us wanted was to have an enjoyable time listening to great country music. The conversation was relaxed and easygoing, and after about an hour of chatting and taking in the scene, I decided to call it a night.

The next morning, I climbed out of bed feeling reenergized. I walked over to the window and drew the curtains back to find another picturesque day awaiting me. *Why not make it all last a little longer?* I asked myself. After all, my daughter was with her mom, so I wouldn't miss any time with her. It was at that moment that I decided to change my return flight from Sunday morning to Monday morning.

I didn't have other plans, and without Alana around, if I returned home, I'd only dive back into my work. Besides, it felt therapeutic to have a break from everything. Returning to work in a better mental space could only be beneficial.

I was having such a good time at the festival, I began to wonder if it was time to start traveling and enjoying life a bit more. I wasn't willing to leave my law firm, but cutting back a bit would give me even more time with Alana, which was especially needed after the types of cases I'd been handling and how mentally and emotionally draining they were. Seeing what happened to those children made me want to be with my daughter as much as I could. I wanted to protect her from the harsh realities of this world in every way possible. I wanted to ensure her childhood was nothing close to mine, and nothing like what the children I represented were forced to endure.

That afternoon, I headed over to the venue around 3:00 p.m., with the intent of staying for only a short while. It was warm outside, so I wore khaki shorts and the festival T-shirt I had purchased the day before. The crowd didn't seem as jam-packed as the night before, but there were thousands of country music fans there. Some were drinking beer, wearing cowboy hats and boots; everyone seemed as relaxed and happy as the previous night.

Jake Owen's barefoot performance ignited the crowd. I'm used to being in courtrooms, arguing my cases, and this ambiance was entirely different. I wanted more, so although I had planned on leaving the concert by 8:00, Jake took the stage and I began to reconsider.

I was seated next to a lovely couple from Austin, Texas, who seemed to feel somewhat bad that I was alone. In between sets, they went out of their way to chat with me. Our pleasant and fluid conversation was a continuation of others I'd had on Saturday. After talking for five or six minutes about my daughter, taking pictures together, and exchanging phone numbers, I found it awkward to leave early. They were genuinely lovely people, so I decided to stay. That choice changed the course of my life forever.

2

Before I knew it, it was 9:40 and Jason Aldean was on stage singing and playing his guitar. Since he was the final act that Sunday night, some of the crowd had already dissipated. I should have headed out as well, but had decided to enjoy a few songs. Suddenly, about thirty minutes into Jason's performance, the air exploded with loud popping sounds. Pop! Pop! Pop! Pop! Confused, people started glancing around and looking up at the dark sky. I thought it might have been fireworks, but I didn't see anything in the sky, so I began to worry.

I noticed the noise had caught Jason's attention, too. He was right in the middle of "When She Says Baby," and seeing him hesitate during his song was unsettling. The look on his face showed that fireworks weren't supposed to be part of his show. He glanced over to his left, but kept singing. Suddenly, there was another round of pops. The atmosphere was no longer celebratory. A chill rolled through the air, making me even more uneasy. Jason paused and I locked my eyes on him. Given his vantage point, if Jason made a move, I decided I needed to follow suit. Then, in a swift response to someone or something he either heard or saw, Jason Aldean tucked his guitar under his armpit and darted off the stage.

I had a sinking feeling something dire was going down, and then it became clear that those popping sounds weren't fireworks—they were gunfire. Complete chaos erupted. At several shots per second, bullets rained down on us. People were running, screaming, frozen, and dropping. It was like we were in a war zone, only we were defenseless, trapped inside barricades.

The firing sent a barrage of bullets ripping through the air with a vengeance, pinging against the metal bleachers, ricocheting off concessions stands and other structures, the cold echo of death. I was terrified. All I could think about was getting shot, dying, and Alana.

The rounds were being fired into the densest part of the audience near the front of the stage. The bullets felt like they were right on top of me. Everything happened so fast that I didn't notice that the couple next to me had fled with the crowd. I ran away from the stage but instinctively dropped to the pavement and stayed there, stock still, praying for the shooting to stop. At six feet tall, I was merely another target.

From the corner of my right eye, I saw a pair of motionless red tennis shoes near me—someone just standing there, an immobile target paralyzed by the terror of it all. Afraid to lift my head, with an outstretched hand, I grabbed hold of the person's beige pant leg and tugged on it, warning them to get down. Quickly, the man dropped to the ground, along with the person next to him. I placed my left hand over my left ear and lay still. My mind flooded with memories of childhood trauma. I felt the cold barrel of my father's gun pressed against my temple while I lay curled in a fetal position on my bed. Once more, I believed I was going to die. And like before, I wanted to get it over with, because the waiting felt unbearable. Panic and high-pitched screams filled the air. That carefree country music scene had become a horrific nightmare.

I was close to the corner of Las Vegas Boulevard near Mandalay Bay. It was impossible to know which way to run. I couldn't tell where the shooting was coming from or how many shooters there were. I thought there must have been multiple gunmen and that they were inside the venue. Running was a gamble I wasn't prepared to take until the shooting paused again or stopped. The cracking of the rapid fire was like nothing I'd ever heard. It sounded like hundreds of bullets at a time were being fired. The manner and duration of the attack made me believe it had been planned.

I lay frozen in fear, watching people rushing to climb over the wire fence about ten feet in front of me. There was no clear way to escape, but they were trying. People were crouched down or huddled together on the sides of concession stands, covering their heads. Some were bereft. Others were heroically carrying the wounded away from what was turning into a graveyard. I saw people shot and injured.

My thoughts began to twist my fear into anger. Why hadn't I kept to my plan and flown back that morning? I'd been alone my whole life, and now I'd die here by myself. My mind was flooded with thoughts of how Alana would remember me, and if people would think I had made a difference with my life. Part of my eulogy raced through my mind. It was dark. I thought I had turned my life around and had been a good father to my daughter, but I wasn't done. I needed to get home to Alana. But at that moment, the worst thing I could do was run. I remained still and waited.

After the next round of fire ceased, I scrambled to my feet, patting my body to check for wounds as I ran a short distance, navigating over scattered shoes, water bottles, personal belongings, broken lawn chairs, and blood, and past bodies. *Dead bodies!*

Suddenly, the shooting resumed. I threw my hands over my head and dropped to the pavement. *This is fucking crazy!* I thought. *The United States is supposed to be a civilized society. This is barbaric. How in the world is this happening? How are they getting these weapons? I can't die here; I have to survive. People can't just get away with this shit.*

At that moment, my anger was interrupted and I felt God's presence. I had a revelation—a spiritual awakening—and everything became clear. My life had meaning, and I had more to do. I wasn't supposed to be here, but I had made the decision to stay one more day. And trying to survive this was teaching me something I'd never forget. I'd had to fight to survive my childhood. I fight for a living, and for some reason, all that fighting prepared me for this. I'd have to fight to get through this, too. "God," I vowed, "if I make it out of here, I'm going to keep fighting for people. I'm going to do *more.*"

The air became eerily calm. There was another pause in the gunfire. I reasoned that maybe the shooters were reloading. This gap seemed longer. A young guy, about five foot six, was bravely waving his hands for me to run into a little space set up like a production area beneath the bleachers. Moments ago, the bullets had been pinging off those same bleachers, but it was more secure than being out in the open. There were six young women in their early twenties, shaking and crying hysterically on their hands and knees. Without thinking, I stood in front of them, trying to protect them. I spotted a six-foot table, grabbed it, and positioned it on its side as a barrier to shield them. I'd want someone to do that for my daughter.

Then another round of fire continued the terror. After assessing my surroundings, I realized I wasn't any safer in my new location. None of us were. We were trapped. If a shooter targeted or came under the bleachers, there was no way out. If there was another pause in the hailstorm of bullets, I had to get out of there. We all did! I was on the edge of the arena.

Hundreds more shots sprayed into the venue, making it impossible to pinpoint where they were coming from. Then, as abruptly as it started, it stopped. All that was left was the sound of screaming and the smell of death permeating the air. I peeked from beneath the bleachers, scouting an area close to a fence on Las Vegas Boulevard just ten feet away. I saw a police officer just outside the venue, approximately fifteen feet from me. When we made eye contact, the police officer pointed and yelled, "Go! Go! Run north now!"

From the onset, each second of gunfire had felt like an hour. Based on the timing of the previous pauses between shootings, I knew we didn't have much time. Maybe seconds. Everyone under the bleachers needed to get out of there, too. I turned around and shouted, "Come on! Get out now! Get out! You've got to get out!" As instructed by the officer, we took off running, fleeing into the mayhem and falling darkness where others had fanned out to find shelter. Escaping the venue evoked the feeling I'd had as a child running barefoot, trying to outrun my brother and father. When trauma is inflicted upon children, it cannot be erased; it can be managed, but the memories are always there.

With bodies sprawled on the ground, and people severely injured, no one cared about shoes, phones, purses, bags, or personal belongings. Like me, they just wanted to survive. They left everything and ran for their lives. I'd seen horror through the eyes of children, but my eyes had never witnessed anything like this. Even when someone explains every detail of abuse they endured, every ounce of pain, and what was taken from them, you cannot understand it until you experience something truly wretched yourself. I understood because I had my own history. Yet this was still sobering. The pandemonium was beyond belief. Thousands of people were trying to flee the venue that moments before had brought them together in peace.

Following a trail of blood, I sprinted away from the stage

toward the Tropicana hotel. Flashing lights, blaring sirens, and dozens of ambulances filled the street. Wounded concertgoers were all over the place. The scene was unreal. People continued to scramble between bursts of gunfire. I felt my back pocket to make sure I hadn't lost my phone—my lifeline to my daughter. I had to call and tell Alana's mother, Susan, what was happening, because if my daughter found out that I was there and that my life was in jeopardy, I needed her to know that, somehow, I'd make it back to her.

Like everyone around me, I was still in an open area, painfully aware that at any moment any one of us could be shot. Until someone stopped this massacre, we were completely vulnerable.

The route to the northbound exit of the concert venue was crowded. Thousands of people heading in the same direction bottlenecked as if gridlocked on the freeway. The piercing screams and deafening hollering that had spilled out of the concert area continued. Scores of people were injured. Others frantically searched for family or friends. The entire scene was devastating. The exit ahead of me, just three or four feet wide, was enough for one or two people to get through at a time. Fear was the only thing causing the congestion, so I started shouting, "One at a time! One at a time!" Every second I waited to get out of there felt like an eternity, as if I were a cow awaiting slaughter.

When I reached the bridge to the Tropicana hotel, I paused, looking back toward the venue. It seemed as if it were miles away. My hands nervously patted down my body once again, confirming that I hadn't been shot. While trying to catch my breath, I reached for my phone and typed a short message to Susan, letting her know about the shooting. I didn't know if anything was happening elsewhere, but I had to find out. Then I sent a text asking Nathalie, a trusted friend and one of the lawyers with my firm, to keep me abreast of any details she could find out. I knew she'd give me the most accurate information. I slid the phone back into my pocket, hustled into the Tropicana through the side entrance, and headed toward the lobby. Finally, I'd reached safety. But just as I was starting to catch my breath, loud screams erupted in my direction, and herds of people trampled past me yelling, "Active shooter! Active shooter in the Tropicana!" The hammering and heaviness revved up again. There was no time. The throngs of people who had forced their way inside now darted through the casino; I followed. Just like at the concert venue, tennis shoes, hats, purses, and cups littered the casino floor. Complete pandemonium. I just wanted it to be over.

I didn't stop running until I came out on the other side of the Tropicana, where I made my way across to an area of large conference rooms at the adjacent MGM hotel. Security from the MGM warned us of their concern that a shooter could come into the hotel. We were advised that if we entered, we would not be allowed to leave. A bunch of us went inside, then security proceeded to lock down the venue and told us to hunker under the tables and hide. They went to work shoring up security in the area until they could determine whether it was safe.

Just like when I was trapped at the concert, it didn't feel like a good idea to have hundreds of people next to each other, crouching under tables. The attack on the venue must have had a deadly impact, because a multitude of us were gathered in one place. Scanning the room, I saw that people were visibly afraid. We waited for answers, or some indication that the nightmare was over. I heard people saying they'd been sent to the conference room from the MGM casino floor. They weren't at the concert, so they didn't know exactly what had happened, just that there was a shooting. I shook my head because they had no idea how bad this was. Given the circumstances and disorder, I felt claustrophobic and unsafe. I needed to get out of there and catch my breath.

Forty-five minutes had passed, and I still didn't know

anything more than what I'd experienced. The sizable conference room was packed, with barely any space to weave through the crowd of people standing, sitting, crouching, leaning against the walls, and comforting one another. I wiped the perspiration from my brow to no avail. The temperature steadily edged its way up, and more beads of sweat formed. As the reign of terror continued, people were frantically texting and making calls to find out what had happened. I wandered the room, my mind filled with images of those who had been killed; it became increasingly difficult to breathe.

Someone unlocked a door, and several people stepped outside to take in the fresh air. I followed so I could gather my thoughts. I heard the blades of helicopters beating the air and looked up to find them hovering in the sky, their bright lights scanning the massacre below. It looked as if the entire city of Las Vegas was under siege. A security guard shouted, "You've got to get back in here, now!" The fifty or so people in the parking lot scrambled to get back inside. Just as I walked through the door, the security guard locked it again.

Somehow, the volume of people in the conference room had increased. Maybe some had come down from the hotel rooms or entered through an exit elsewhere. It was hard to tell, but the conference room swarmed with clusters of new faces appearing anxious or scared. They may have been separated from someone, or alone like me.

I made my way from the conference room into the wide but overcrowded hallway. People squeezed through the crowd, pleading in hushed voices, "Quiet down. We have to be quiet." Two couples in their late twenties asked me if I knew what was going on. They had been in the MGM casino after attending a hockey game and didn't know anything other than that a shooting had occurred. After sharing the graveness of the situation, we discussed options. There were two factors to consider: what had already happened, and the unknown. We agreed none of us felt safe in such a large gathering. One of the men quietly slipped away to search for a less crowded place to hide. When he returned a few minutes later, he told us he'd found the entrance to a kitchen farther down the hallway. The four of us followed him. It didn't seem much safer, but no one else was in there.

Waiting helplessly in the MGM kitchen, we plotted how we might get out of there and off the Strip. One of the guys asked me to reach out to my contacts to find out what was going on, and to keep the girls safe while he and the other man ventured off to find another exit—one that led to the street. I sent texts to both Susie and Nathalie, asking them to search the news and determine what was going on. It turned out there was a lot of misinformation circulating that didn't match at all what I'd experienced. There was also a report of a shooting at another casino, and I didn't know what was factual, what the shooters' motives were, or if we were hiding inside the next target.

Minutes later, the guys returned and confirmed they'd found a way out. After sharing the information I'd gotten, we agreed to wait a while longer, hoping things would have time to settle. When we made our move, we'd make it together. Until then, I'd remain hypervigilant, but optimistic that time would allow the police to capture whoever was responsible. I texted Susie again and she explained that the media was saying that the major casinos in Las Vegas were on lockdown. It didn't alleviate our concern for the state of things, but we had no recourse other than to be patient.

Forty-five minutes later, we decided it was time to run for it. Clustered together, we scurried through the door and ran for what seemed like an eternity to go an eighth of a mile to the lot where one of the men had parked his car. The MGM was on lockdown, and as far as we knew, the entire city was, too. As we pulled off, Nathalie began texting me updates on what the news was reporting.

It turned out that both couples I was with lived in Henderson, Nevada. They could have found their way out of the city, but my belongings were still at the hotel. The driver circled the area looking for a street that wasn't closed off, and in the meantime, I tried to figure out where I should go. Mandalay Bay wasn't an option, and trying to catch a flight home didn't feel right. I couldn't just leave the city and the people who'd lost loved ones while we were all still struggling to understand why it had happened.

When my phone buzzed, I was relieved to see it was a text from the couple from Austin I'd sat next to at the concert. They were safe and checking to see if I had made it out. When I told the wife I couldn't go back to my hotel, she sent the name of the hotel they were staying at on the outskirts of Vegas and invited me to stay with them. I asked the driver to drop me off there. Since the streets were shut down, we could only get within a half mile of that hotel. Before pulling off, the couples thanked me for my help and told me to be safe. I told them not to stop driving until they found their way home.

The warm air had long dissipated, and I found myself trekking wearily along the side of the highway, alone and in complete darkness. Attempting to find the hotel, I held on to the thought that each step took me farther away from death. I contemplated my future and what I was meant to do. I had heard God loud and clear—and I understood.

In my spiritual awakening, I discovered that this is what it's like for children in this country and around the world every single day. Children are not in a position to defend themselves. The power dynamics remove their voices, allowing abuse to remain an epidemic. Instead of dialing back on my work, I would rededicate myself. The events of this one day convinced me beyond a doubt that I should continue doing what I knew how to do best—fight.

3

It was around 3:00 a.m. when I walked into the lobby of the hotel and called the couple who had been seated next to me at the concert. I let them know I had arrived safely, and that while I appreciated their offer to share their room, I would get one of my own rather than impose on them. A moment later, I started receiving messages from my publicist asking if I was okay. As part of my job, I was a regular national television legal commentator on Fox News, CNN, CNN International, HLN, and *Good Morning America*, among others.

Eventually, my phone's battery died. I managed to borrow a charger from a gentleman at the front desk, and while my phone charged, I sat in the lobby and attempted to regroup. As soon as there was enough battery life, messages started rolling in and my phone rang. Someone from *Good Morning America* (*GMA*) had heard that I was at the festival, and they wanted to talk to me. It was 7:00 a.m. in New York and they were about to go on air. I did my best to collect myself and did a fifteen-minute phone interview where I gave my account of what happened. Reliving the horror I'd just experienced was traumatic. After that conversation, my publicist called and asked if I could meet up with the crew from *GMA*, and I agreed. As difficult as it was to relive the horrifying memories, I wanted everyone to know what had just happened, and I wanted them to care.

I was three miles away from Mandalay Bay, and *GMA* was going to send a car to pick me up and take me there after an interview. I went down the street to the 7-Eleven, bought a phone charger, and returned to the hotel lobby just as the car pulled up to take me to the interview. It was dark, cold, and windy. When I did the interview, I was still wearing the blue Route 91 T-shirt I'd had on during the shooting. It wasn't until then that I started to learn the extent of the devastation, the name of the killer, and that he had operated from inside the Mandalay Bay. Eventually, law enforcement confirmed that the gunman had murdered 60 people and wounded 411 others before killing himself.

As I recounted what had transpired to *GMA*'s Robin Roberts, I broke down. Images from that night flashed in my head while I spoke. When the media talks about a tragedy, they have a way of making things seem orderly, because they see an event logically, from the outside, while participants actually experience it emotionally. They could interview a thousand people and everyone's account would be different. For me, the situation wasn't orderly—it was traumatic, chaotic, and devastating.

I finished the interview and wanted nothing more in that moment than to return to my hotel. A *GMA* representative dropped me off about a half mile away from Mandalay Bay. There must have been dozens of reporters from every show possible interviewing people. The scene was mayhem. Local reporters were everywhere.

My publicist contacted me again, and I ended up doing an interview with a reporter from a Las Vegas station, and another with CNN's Chris Cuomo. When I went to that interview, I met a gentleman named Bryan Hopkins, the lead singer for Elvis Monroe. For the next twenty-four hours, Bryan and I would shadow each other, giving interview after interview. After that, I somehow knew that we had become lifelong friends. Over the next few hours, as the details of what had happened continued to unfold, I became visibly ill. I can see it when I look back at those interviews. Stephen Paddock had murdered innocent people, destroyed countless lives, and traumatized others, myself included.

As horrible as I felt, I still wasn't ready to leave. I felt pain and a connection to what happened. I needed to stay and be around other survivors; it didn't feel right to abandon them. After learning more details about the shooter, Stephen Paddock, how he'd been situated in a room at the hotel, and the extent of the devastation he'd caused, I did everything possible to wrap my mind around it all. It was senseless. I was in shock. I wanted to go back to the scene of the crime for proof that it had happened, but I knew I wouldn't be able to get anywhere near the venue.

When I got back to Mandalay Bay, I was shocked to see that there were folks in the casino, playing the slots and roulette as if nothing had happened. Walking through the lobby, all I heard was "Wheel—of—Fortune! Ching, ching, ching . . ." How on earth was this possible?

Around noon, I rode the hotel elevator to the twenty-sixth floor with Matt Gutman, a national television correspondent with *Good Morning America*. He joined me to get a vantage point on the shooting aftermath. During the anxiety-ridden elevator ride, I pondered whether we were on the same elevator that Paddock had taken with all his weapons. It didn't feel safe, because I didn't see any police or security. They seemed to be acting as if everything was fine.

Stepping off the elevator, I saw that nothing was taped off, so I went to my room. I looked out the window, glancing to the left and just a few floors up to Paddock's room. The windows had been blown out, and the curtains were blowing. When I turned and looked across to the concert venue, I was taken aback to see the mass carnage of the crime scene. Yet downstairs, inside the hotel, people were still gambling, music blaring and all. The casino should have been a massive crime scene, but Mandalay Bay was open, and people went on as if they didn't know or care what had happened.

I used my phone to take pictures from my window to validate for myself what had happened, and what I saw made everything more real. I was bewildered. It was such a contradiction to smell so much death while the world around me was festive. Then my phone vibrated. It was a message from the hotel. *Given "the disturbance" that happened, if you'd like to stay an extra night, please let us know.* The worst mass shooting in American history had just occurred, and the hotel was offering to comp our rooms for a night. No apology. No show of genuine concern.

I hadn't slept in twenty-four hours. Memories of trying to escape the venue overtook me, catapulting me back to when I was a teenager, running barefoot on a snowy street to escape my brother and father. It was as if their hateful acts and the fear they caused had been replicated and magnified. No one could save me, so my struggles and pain continued.

4

Finally, it was time to return home. When I boarded my flight on Tuesday, I was still wearing the shorts and T-shirt I'd worn at the concert. I was out of disposable contact lenses, and I hadn't slept or eaten since the massacre.

On the short flight home, it all started to catch up with me. I felt weighed down by mental exhaustion, physical fatigue, and survivor's guilt. I realized that I was no longer the same man. Part of my soul had died in the shooting. I would never again see the world the same or feel the way I had prior to the shooting. Surviving the massacre had stirred up the buried fears from my childhood and left me helpless, not knowing how to process and handle it. I was a trial lawyer, not a therapist, and I needed help.

Inhaling deeply, I slipped the key into my front door and released a heavy sigh. Crossing the threshold of my home in Pasadena, I felt safe, but somehow worse. I'd had to hold everything in to focus on survival, then act like normal until I got back to Pasadena. Being home meant I could let out everything I was holding in. The stench of death, the smell of fear, the horrifying expressions of terrified concertgoers, the cracking of bullets, the screams, and the crying.

I wanted to see my daughter, but not in that shape. Alana still didn't know that I had been in the massacre, and I wasn't ready to tell her. I didn't want her to worry. At that moment, I had to shut down to deal with it. There was nothing left in me.

The next few days were the same: intense thoughts and an emptiness in my chest. I couldn't bring myself to go back to my life as if nothing had happened. Just as everything played out in my head, it played out all over the news, causing me to plunge into a dark hole. I isolated myself in my home.

By the second week, I still hadn't seen anyone from my office, and I wasn't ready to go back to work, but Nathalie thought it would be beneficial for me to get out of the house. A couple of days later, I met her at a Subway restaurant in a historic part of Pasadena. I was trying to make a concerted effort to stay current on our cases and business as a whole, yet being out in the open made me uncomfortable. Screeching brakes startled me. A car backfired, and I wanted to dive under the table.

At Subway, I observed a guy sitting at a booth eating. Another guy, wearing a tan-and-olive camouflage jacket, stood up and placed his right hand inside his jacket as though he were reaching for something. Without thinking, and without a word to Nathalie, I darted out of the restaurant. I thought he was pulling out a gun. The flashback had me grabbing my chest, gasping for air. I felt like I was right back at the shooting. Even in my community, I couldn't manage to feel safe outside in a social setting. Nathalie was completely understanding when I told her I just needed to go home.

This wasn't me, and I didn't want to be this way, but I was damaged. Before the shooting, I was noticeably outgoing and, I thought, pretty funny at times. I could be in the middle of talking about something and easily break out with a joke. I'd gotten that slice of my personality from my Italian mother, who was affable and engaging, and her family. The change in me was profound. When you experience something as horrifying and unnatural as a mass murder, it takes up residence in your mind, dampening your humor and your happiness. Survivor's guilt began to wipe out any joy I felt. Suddenly, taking a shower, cooking, or keeping a scheduled session with my therapist was difficult. I stopped going to the gym to avoid being around people. Whenever I left the house, I wanted to get back home as quickly as possible. It was the only place I felt safe. Driving on the freeway was stressful. In Los Angeles, traffic bottlenecks. There always seemed to be a car on each side of me, behind me, and in front of me. I felt boxed in—the way I had at the massacre. Frequently, I'd have to exit the freeway and pull off the road to catch my breath and pray. Being at a stoplight was difficult. My preference became taking stairs rather than elevators, which created immense anxiety. I didn't want to be closed in and lose all control.

This went on for many months. I had to constantly recalibrate my brain and remind myself that I was no longer at the concert.

At one point, my pastor, Jim Reeve, asked me to share my account of the shooting at a service. Considering that it was my faith that had carried me through, I felt compelled to offer my testimony. Although I was grateful to be alive, I wasn't in the best place mentally. How could I be? It was still hard to process the fact that Mandalay Bay's failed security had enabled Stephen Paddock to murder all those innocent people.

I went back to church and delivered an emotional testimony during the Sunday service. As I heard the words flow from my lips, I realized how incredibly blessed I was and knew there was a process I had to work through before I could heal. The shooting was magnified and challenging to overcome because it released the suppressed memories of abuse lodged deep inside me.

I discovered that each of us is unique in our experiences and responds uniquely to mass trauma. Mentally, I wanted the world to stop and have a halftime for a few months so I could get back to normal, but it kept moving. The reality is that there is never enough time to comfort those who have survived a mass trauma, or any trauma. My daughter still needed me, my cases were mounting, and I had personal obligations. Aware that life goes on, I put the idea of reconciling my memories and feelings around my childhood abuse, along with what I'd just experienced, on hold.

Still, I felt a drive to help others. I had an internal prompt or calling to do something for the Las Vegas victims, and I could do that safely from home. Along with fellow Las Vegas survivor Lisa Fine, I started a nonprofit, Route 91 Strong, and ended up raising $150,000 for victims. Most of the people we assisted had post-traumatic stress disorder (PTSD). Several of them couldn't go back to work or had lost their jobs. Through our nonprofit, we were able to help a lot of victims pay rent, make their mortgage payments, and cover essential bills. It felt right, and I was glad we did it, but the downside was that it thwarted my recovery process. While I was working to help others, I wasn't tackling my own issues. While others were attempting to work through their trauma, Lisa and I tabled our issues and made other victims a priority. And while I attempted to move forward, each victim we helped repeatedly took me back there. Their trauma ran deep, and the conversations kept mine fresh.

After the shooting, I allowed myself to get buried in the feeling of being overwhelmed because I didn't know how to stop it. My mind was consumed with the shooting.

As a lawyer, I was used to multitasking, but suddenly it had become difficult to do. It was so bad that I needed to write notes on pieces of paper and put the paper on the floor by the door to remind myself to do basic tasks. I was suffocated by the daily responsibilities of life and had to learn how to separate and compartmentalize different obligations. I'd write down what I had to do, subdividing each specific task, writing down things as basic as going to the store. Prior to the shooting, I could easily juggle fifteen different things. In the midst of a frenzy, my brain was free to roam and be spontaneous, generating solutions and ideas. I still had that aptitude when it came to work, but when it came to my personal life, I was lost. I'd never had to write down the things I needed to do. But now I had to consciously record my responsibilities for each moment, before they got washed away by the hurricane in my head.

Eventually, I was able to engage in therapy, and that process helped me deal with some of the trauma. I also leaned heavily on my church and my faith.

Post-shooting, my view of the world has changed. Trauma affects people differently, but you can't escape it. After a natural disaster, there is the aftermath. With trauma, whether it's violence; sexual abuse; or physical, mental, or emotional abuse, there will be consequences. I am empathetic to and understand the things my clients go through to suppress adverse history. Holding on to secrets, abusing drugs, pain and suffering, sleep disturbances, lack of trust, promiscuity, suicide attempts, eating disorders, passiveness, and helplessness—these are all normal. I've experienced some of them myself and have seen countless others travel these roads as well.

My journey placed me in a senseless massacre—after an abusive and neglectful childhood—but it also brought me to understand most deeply why I fight for others. There is a greater responsibility. It's a moral responsibility. And I do more than represent them legally; I also support their souls. Through empathy and comprehension, I help them with their process. I aim to advocate for my clients—adults, children, parents, and the deceased. And I work to change the organizations that need change.

PART II

THE TRAUMA CYCLE

5

Sometimes trauma comes from a sudden senseless event, like the Las Vegas massacre. Other times, it's the result of ongoing abuse. And sometimes, not infrequently, it's part of a cycle in which a victim of abuse goes on to become a perpetrator. Growing up, I was part of that cycle.

Both my parents were in the military. In 1949, Ramona Marzano-Claypool served in one of the first female regiments of the US Marine Corps. She was beautiful and intelligent, and most of all, she cared deeply about people. The marines sent Ramona across the country on recruiting trips, and I was told she met Charles W. Claypool—a tall, handsome physical specimen—at an event in Southern California. Charles ended up serving twenty-five years in the army and marine corps, and as fate would have it, they became my parents.

I was born in Latrobe, Pennsylvania. Shortly after, we moved to Fort Meade, Maryland, then relocated to an American army base in Babenhausen, Germany, where I attended kindergarten and most of the first grade. Our last move was back to Lawson Heights, Pennsylvania, a small town with rolling hills, four miles from downtown Latrobe.

A stone arch bridge took us across the Loyalhanna Creek into Latrobe. That bridge was significant to me because crossing it was like entering a different world. I thought the viaduct took me to someplace better—away from where the worst memories of my childhood were formed.

Lawson Heights was a blue-collar town in a middle-class neighborhood, near Latrobe Steel and Kennametal. At the time, both were major steel resources for the military, and during WWII, their presence put Latrobe on the top of a short list of places that would likely be targeted if the States were bombed. If you worked at either the steel mills or the Rolling Rock brewery, you were a celebrity.

Lawson Heights was a beautiful area surrounded by lush, rolling hills. The historic church we attended—Saint Vincent Basilica—was in the Romanesque revival architectural style. It sat on a hill and was visible from our front yard. Saint Vincent College had a sprawling athletic complex, and the Pittsburgh Steelers practiced there during the summer.

Looking out from our front yard, to the right was a massive cornfield that I played in with my friends around Halloween. To the left, you could see the majestic Laurel Highlands, and straight ahead the Latrobe airport. When golf tournaments at the local country club ended on Sunday, people would turn to the sky to watch legendary golfer Arnold Palmer fly his plane back home to Latrobe. It seemed that practically everyone in town knew that Arnold Palmer's airplane was the small six-passenger one with the distinctly loud engine.

My parents, two sisters, brother, and I lived in a split-level house with one bathroom, a small kitchen, a living room, and two small bedrooms upstairs. The lower level was supposed to be a den so we could watch television, but Dad divided that room and made one side into a makeshift bedroom that my older brother, Charles, and I shared until my older sister moved out and I took her bed in the room upstairs.

I like to think that my parents were happy at some point, but I have no warm memories of them being close. Instead, my earliest recollections are of them screaming and yelling at one another. Charles and I could hear the commotion from our downstairs bedroom. I'd sneak up the stairs and peek around the corner to find Dad chasing Mom around the dining table while she was throwing things at him to protect herself. Sometimes it was the other way around.

Dad would often disappear for three or four days at a time. I never knew when or if he was coming home—he could have been at someone's house, in an accident, or dead. It caused me a great deal of anxiety, yet at the same time, there were many nights I hoped he *wouldn't* come home, because inevitably, when he came in late, it was a disaster. If he wasn't home before ten o'clock, I'd go to bed tense and restless. When he finally did arrive, he'd announce himself by slamming the door. *The Major's home!* He'd bang things around, pound on the counter, and scream, "Where's my fucking food!" At that time of night, I should have been sound asleep, but instead, I lay awake, flooded with fear. I never knew when or if I'd fall asleep. School nights were even more stressful because sleep or no, I'd have to drag myself out of bed the next morning and somehow manage to get through the day.

Sometimes when Dad was out, Mom would scoop me up and quietly sit me on her lap. I'd rest my head on her breast as she comforted me, and I felt loved and safe. But in that house, nothing good seemed to last.

The worst was when Mom got sick. No one ever told me that anything was wrong. Suddenly, the loving, nurturing woman who'd been so active in our community stopped being herself and spent a lot of time in bed. I'd wander into her bedroom and glimpse the bottles on her nightstand—four or five little orange containers filled with white pills. She never told me why she'd started taking them; she just slept.

One day after school, I went home and found Mom sitting in a recliner. I climbed on her lap, but she was weak and could barely manage to hold me. I could tell something was different, then realized one of her breasts was no longer there. I sat silently, leaning against her, trying my best not to let her see my shock. I didn't know what had happened; I'd never heard about breast cancer. Shortly after, the other breast was gone, too. The place I'd rested my head for comfort was gone.

I don't have many memories of Mom before she had cancer, mostly just the way she held me. It felt like the cancer took my mother's love away from me. At the time, doctors didn't do breast reconstruction after mastectomies, so Mom stayed that way.

No one sat me down and explained what was going on or helped me handle things. I didn't understand. All I knew was that breast cancer was an ugly, vile disease, and it had turned my mom into a monster. It took most of her hair, leaving thin strands that ran from the top of her nearly bare scalp down to her neck. Jaundice turned the whites around her desolate brown eyes to a dull yellow. Her body always had an unpleasant odor tinged with the smell of urine. She had a horrendous cough. She'd hack and gasp painfully for air, often causing her to urinate on the couch, chairs, and her bed. Daily, my younger sister Patricia and I—the only kids still living at home—had to clean up after her.

Dad was barely around. My sister Colleen, who had moved out of the house to live with her boyfriend, stopped by when she could. She and Dad were not on good terms, and her decision to move out alienated her from the household. Still, once in a while Colleen would stop by when Dad wasn't around and would help with the cleaning and other work that needed to be done. But Trish and I handled the lion's share.

It was rough. Trying to follow Mom's dietary restrictions, we cooked bland foods. As time passed and Mom's appetite declined, we would just heat a can of soup. We administered her medications on a regular schedule and kept the house clean. We never talked with Mom about her illness, or much of anything else, for that matter. But I knew she appreciated everything we did for her—I could always see the gratitude in her eyes. Finally, Mom went into remission, and I breathed a sigh of relief.

Growing up, there were bright spots in my life, such as visiting my mother's parents. Mom's father, Grandfather Marzano, had owned a farm in Bari, Italy, but he decided to try to make a life for his family in America. He left his wife in Italy and moved to Rochester, New York, where he started a tailor shop. Once he was set up, he brought her over, and they lived together happily in a modest house.

I have fond memories of visiting them and smelling the bread dough in their home. My grandmother would wrap the dough in a freezer bag so there was room for it to expand, then sit it on the corner of the sofa, waiting for it to rise. When it was ready, we'd watch her make homemade pizza from the dough. I felt safe there, and enjoyed a sense of culture and family, especially when they spoke Italian.

Being with my grandparents was an escape for me, and I was always sad when we returned to Latrobe and the chaos that awaited us. There, I felt homeless within a home.

A weekly escape to Lincoln Lanes also helped me manage the stress of my parents' fighting and my father's aggression and erratic behavior. I was so desperate to escape my home that even in the winter months, I carried my red bowling bag and twelve-pound ball, which I'd bought with earnings from my paper route, nearly two miles each way. I'd had the holes drilled into the ball to make sure my fingers fit perfectly.

It took about forty-five minutes to walk to the bowling alley along Route 30, and once I got there, I'd settle down in front of the heaters. It would take an hour to thaw out my hands and feet enough that I could bowl. Then I'd practice my technique, working on keeping my swing relaxed and lining up my shot. Focusing on the details took me away from everything that was happening at home, and it paid off in my skill level. When I was twelve, I won an award for having a three-game series of 623 pins, which meant I bowled three games of 200 or above. It was one of the best scores in our region or state.

My parents didn't see me bowl and never knew how good I became, but excelling at something like that, applying myself and seeing results, was one of the best experiences of my young life. I was shrouded in negativity, and bowling was a ray of light—a sliver of something good that carried me through difficult times. It's no exaggeration to say that bowling, along with playing basketball at the playground, helped me survive. My being at the bowling alley and the playground, spending all that time alone and withdrawn into myself, was one of countless red flags that something was wrong. I was lucky that in all that time, no one took advantage of the fact that I was by myself by abducting or otherwise harming me.

Sports and activities are great for children, but when they are engaging in activities seemingly to escape their homelife, that is a concern. If a child appears to have a lack of confidence or low self-esteem, someone or something is causing them to behave that way, which can be a sign that they are being bullied or verbally abused. Alternatively, if a child is a bully, that can indicate that the child is being bullied or

subjected to abuse. Also, depending on the environment, if you see children walking near and around businesses or parking lots alone, know that those are perfect places for them to be harmed. We have to be more responsible as adults and notice these things. That alone could save lives or prevent children from being abducted.

Sometimes Patricia and I would walk a mile to Dairy Queen to get ice cream. We'd get Mom a little scoop of vanilla in a cup and hurry back before it melted. That was the highlight of any Sunday evening.

Yet just as things seemed like they were starting to normalize, the atmosphere at home shifted and became darker—Mom's cancer returned. At that time, the belief was that if you made it five years without the cancer reoccurring, there was a chance you'd survive, but Mom's came back after four.

It was devastating to see Mom suffering again, and this round was even worse. I'd cringe when I heard her dry, painful cough echo throughout the house, because I knew Mom was hurting and because it was like a distress call, signaling that Trish and I would have to go and help her. We did everything we could for Mom, including bathing her. We went back to changing her sheets, washing the linen, and cleaning the furniture, just like before. When it was time for Mom to take her medicine, I'd sort through the bottles of pills, making sure I was giving her the right one. I also monitored to make sure that when we were at school, she was taking her pills on schedule.

Though Mom had battled cancer before, this time, the changes in her appearance were even more drastic. She grew thin, but her body became bloated and her stomach distended. When she wore a one-piece nightgown, her belly looked like a medicine ball, hard and round. The jaundice returned, coloring her feet and eyes an even darker yellow tinge, and the medication tinged her breath with a strong, foul odor.

My sister and I weren't aware that the cancer had metastasized and that Mom was in a terminal state, but I knew something awful was happening. For some reason, I held out hope. Even when her movements became measured and limited, I somehow thought she'd get better. Maybe it was because Mom tried so hard to make us believe that she would. In spite of evidence to the contrary, I needed to believe her. I lived in a state of denial. It was unfathomable that my mother would die. The thought of being left alone in that house with my father was terrifying. So I suppressed it. Odd as it may seem, the thought of actually losing my mother never crossed my mind. Mom was just the way she was, and Trish and I took good care of her. We were handling it.

Mom could barely walk as far as the front yard, so my sister and I went to the grocery store and did the shopping. Strangely, no one ever questioned why two young kids were suddenly doing all the family's grocery shopping or why my mother looked the way she did. Reflecting back, it was a puzzle that was painfully easy to solve, yet no one took the time or the effort to engage. To ask where our parents were and whether everything was okay. I'm not sure how we'd have responded, but between Trish and me always being out on our own, my mom's illness and subsequent disappearance from daily life, and my dad's volatile behavior, it was obvious that something was terribly wrong. It wouldn't have taken much to reach out to the police and suggest that they check in on us.

If a parent is hospitalized for any reason, or being treated for a major medical issue, the hospital, physician, or someone else should be responsible for checking on the children left in the home to make sure they have another parent or guardian taking care of them.

When uncomfortable things are happening in the home or elsewhere, children are good indicators that something is wrong. Pay attention to their responses to questions and their behaviors. Are they fearful, withdrawn, or nervous? Question what does not seem right.

When my father did come home, he expected the house to be clean and organized, so we did our best to keep it that way. We did the laundry and anything we thought Mom typically handled before her illness, so she wouldn't worry and he wouldn't be upset. I also didn't really have any choice but to keep our clothes washed, because we didn't have much to wear.

As Mom's health deteriorated, she moved out of the bedroom she shared with Dad and slept in another twin bed in Trish's room. She was lethargic and sedentary. If she wasn't sleeping, I'd often find her lying on the bed staring at the ceiling. There wasn't much Trish and I could do for her. Periodically, we'd help her out of bed and walk her out to the living room and help her settle on the olive-green velvety sofa, where she'd remain for long periods. That was Mom's life.

When she spoke, it was mostly to say, "Thank you for

helping me," in what sounded like a painful whisper. Even at that point, she still went out of her way to keep us from worrying over her health, trying to shield us from her dire situation. We were just children. We didn't know that cancer was silently killing our mother. It was tormenting to see my mother cry, even without understanding the totality of her illness, the pain it caused, and the loneliness she must have felt. At one point she told me it saddened her that Trish and I were spending our childhoods taking care of her. When she spoke, her face was awash in guilt and embarrassment, as if she'd done something wrong.

Taking care of Mom didn't bother me—it was Dad's behavior that was upsetting. His appearances at home were sporadic, and when he was there, he didn't lift a finger to take care of her. I didn't know if he didn't want to help his wife or if he just didn't know what to do, but every time I checked, her medication was always still there. He couldn't even manage to give her a dose of pills. Nevertheless, my sister and I would always figure things out.

I'd grown used to taking care of Mom. I never felt anger or resentment over the fact that during her fight with cancer, I couldn't do much with my friends. Without Trish and me, she would have been alone. She needed us.

After chemo, Mom's decline was swift. Having insulated myself from the inevitable outcome, it came as a surprise.

One day, I was out on my paper route. Lawson Heights was a sprawling area, so regardless of the weather, I had to walk several miles to deliver the newspapers. During the four years when Mom was in remission, she'd helped me fold the newspapers, count the money, and wrap a rubber band around the papers. Now, I was doing it all on my own. I had just delivered a paper to a local beer store at the shopping center in town when I was surprised to see Colleen pull up in her boyfriend's silver Gran Torino. She'd been looking for me to tell me that our mother had died.

"Get in the car," Colleen said as I stared at her, dumbfounded. A chill raced through my body; it numbed every part of me. I had given my mother as much of my time as possible, and still, in the end, I wasn't there to say goodbye. I never thought Mom would actually leave me.

"Get in the car," Colleen repeated.

6

It's not like I didn't have any semblance of a normal family. I did. And it was there until it wasn't.

My siblings and I were raised as staunch Catholics. Even Dad attended church with us until the first time Mom became ill. My mother was an exceptionally kind and generous woman, and her faith was so strong that she continued taking us to church until she couldn't physically manage. On Sundays, catechism came before watching football, and we knew we were expected to be there for the Rosary. That was one of the gifts my mom gave me—planting the seed for a relationship with God. Then one spring day, a few days after Colleen had tracked me down on my paper route, we gathered to say goodbye to my mother at Saint Vincent's.

The pews stretched back probably forty rows or more. I sat next to my sisters in a pair of nice shorts, a collared shirt, and tennis shoes. Suddenly, in the middle of the service, the realization hit me and I couldn't breathe. All of this was for my mother. My mother was never coming back.

I became completely hysterical. Tears poured from my soul and streamed down my face. I jumped out of my seat and ran for the doors, screaming and crying down the church steps. I reached the sidewalk, turned left, and ran down the hill for at least half a mile, only to stop when I could no longer breathe. She was dead. *Gone.*

No one prepared us for the inevitability of my mother's death. And after all the time and effort I had put in to make sure she was okay, I felt betrayed. I had done everything I could to keep my mother with us. Neither she nor my father told me, or even alluded to the possibility, that she was going to die. Didn't she realize that without her there, I would have to fend for myself? How could she think that I could take being in that house without her? The least she could do was try to prepare me.

It was hard enough losing Mom, but when Dad returned to the house, life became even worse. I had stayed so busy taking care of Mom, doing everything I could to keep from losing her, that I'd blocked out Dad and the disdain he had for me. For years, I repressed my pain by focusing on my mother; it was the only way I could function in that environment. But now that Mom was gone, everything changed.

The entire time Mom was ill, Dad had been having extramarital affairs. I was a child, but I saw the way my father was living. When I delivered the papers early in the morning, I'd see Dad's car parked in a neighbor lady's driveway. She lived just a quarter mile from our house. Sometimes I'd see Dad driving in the car with her, or I'd see her drive by and leave a note for Dad in our mailbox. I never told Mom because there was no point in making things worse for someone already in pain.

At least it kept him out of the house. As long as Mom was around, his abusive tendencies were more verbal and emotional. After she passed, he didn't care where we were, what we had to eat, or if we had clothing.

We went days without seeing Dad. If he wasn't working, he

was hanging out at the Sheraton bar or right off the highway on Route 30 at Mr. P's in Greensburg. Mr. P's wasn't like the Sheraton; it was dark and dingy. When Dad took me there, I didn't have a good feeling about that place, but seeing him intoxicated made me decide not to drink. Somehow it made me want to be better and do better.

People assume that home is the healthiest place for children, but it wasn't for me. No one knew what was going on behind closed doors, but the warning signs that something was wrong were present for anyone who cared to see them. My father routinely frequented bars, and it would have been impossible not to suspect he had a problem. Everyone who knew him knew he was a single dad with two young children at home. Who was home with the kids? Anyone at the bar could have asked him that question. When he was having his affair, the lady was complicit in Dad's neglect. She knew we were alone after Mom passed.

Dad always left empty bottles around wherever he finished them, and he didn't care to hide his drunkenness at home, so I doubt he hid it anywhere else. People knew. But they neglected to advocate for us or question our situation.

If you regularly see a single parent of young children at a bar drinking, that could be a sign that the children are being abandoned. Call the child abuse hotline or social services to do a wellness check.

My father was what they call a functional alcoholic. He could miss a day of work, then show up the second half of the following day and somehow catch up on everything. Sometimes Trish and I would come home from school and his office would call looking for him.

"Is your dad there?"

My standard reply was "No, he's out and about." It's what Dad told me to say to cover for him, and it was my first experience of the code of silence. "What happens at home stays at home," and "Our business is ours and no one else's," Dad would say. But I felt uncomfortable lying for him.

One of the reasons people overlooked Dad's behavior was his status within the community. After he got out of the military, he became the administrator of Latrobe Hospital, and later served as the county administrator for the Westmoreland County Mental Health and Retardation Center. Subsequently, Dad was elected the Westmoreland County administrator for the Children's Bureau. Dad's name was prominent in our community because of his military background and civilian work as an elected official. Once people knew who he was, it seemed it didn't matter what he did, it was all overlooked.

Like so many of us, my father was a complex person with a complex history. He grew up in a low-income neighborhood on the south side of Pittsburgh. His father died when he was young, leaving his mother to care for him. But instead of nurturing her son, she rejected him, letting it be known that she was ashamed of him. She routinely berated my father, going so far as to try and hide him away from the world, literally. When the man she was dating would come over, she would lock my father in a closet for hours at a time. Often, he was left to fend for himself, roaming the streets of Pittsburgh, stealing food to survive.

Understandably, my father couldn't wait to leave home. When he was about twelve or thirteen, he lied about his age to get a job in a local bakery. He was as much interested in making money as he was in having access to food. When he was just fifteen, he lied about his age again and joined the merchant marine.

Growing up, I didn't understand all the war stories Dad told us, but there was one that clearly made a deep impact on him. He told me he was on a ship heading to war—I believe it was the Korean War. Two ships, including his, were heading out on Christmas Eve. Suddenly, there was an attack, and he witnessed the one next to him get blown up. Everyone on that ship died; some of them were his friends. Every Christmas Eve, his behavior would become especially erratic. He'd get drunk and verbally abusive, so we never really enjoyed a peaceful Christmas Eve as kids. Oftentimes we opened our gifts on Christmas Day without Dad because he was recovering from his alcoholic rages. Burdened with survivor's guilt, Dad had trauma, PTSD perhaps. I don't know for sure, but whatever it was, he didn't know how to manage it, and he never received any counseling or support from the military. When he retired, there was no help to transition to civilian life.

One thing I've learned is that nearly all the people who become perpetrators of abuse or violence have undiagnosed mental health issues. Dad needed help, and he didn't get it. In that way, it's like he was victimized twice over. As a result, he continued the cycle of abuse.

My father had his strengths, and there was a lot to like about him; in many ways he inspired me. He became a major by twenty-nine years old and retired when he was approaching forty. He never finished high school, yet he had a thirst for knowledge and worked hard to be successful after the military. It was one of his more admirable traits, and one that stayed with me.

My father was a tenacious and resourceful researcher. If there was something he needed to know, he went to the library and read everything he could find about it. That's how he managed to obtain such a high degree of professional success in spite of his lack of formal education. As horrible as my father was to me at times, I admired that about him. He was truly a self-made man.

He was highly respected for his intelligence and how he presented himself. Somehow, despite his alcoholism, he always managed to put himself together, wearing a crisp sport coat. Dad's bedroom was always organized, and when he dressed for work, he pulled it off, looking polished and pressed with his jacket and shined shoes. I liked the fact that Dad dressed well. Even today, I emulate Dad through my style of dress. He kept the physical bearing of someone in the military and would routinely remind me to correct my posture. I have many memories of walking down the street to the park, and as I headed off, Dad would lean out the window shouting, "Straighten up those shoulders!" Years later, when I was standing in front of a jury arguing my case, I was grateful to my father for teaching me how to present myself.

Despite his behavior at home, it seemed Dad was making a difference in the community, and in many ways, I believe he did. Still, as a kid I didn't understand Dad's personality. At one point before Mom died, I was told that he didn't want to be married to her, which was why he stayed away from home. It was terrible, but it helped me understand him and his absence a bit better. I also discovered that he resented us because in the military he had been a major, and his next appointment was to lieutenant colonel, but he retired before he received it, apparently because of his obligation to his family.

Even though he was my father, there was a lot I didn't know about him. Since I didn't have a healthy relationship with him and we didn't talk about a lot of things, I only knew what I experienced and observed, and the bits and pieces he told us here and there. I know that what I saw wasn't all there was to Dad. Of course there was more, and it could have all been amazing, but I didn't get to see the other parts of him. Instead, I got what he thought I deserved. We hardly ever spoke about his life or experiences, or my school or sports. He never had "the talk" with me or wanted to hear about any of my goals. All I ever heard was "You better join the ROTC." He wanted me to have the same success in the military that he'd had.

Ironically, in his role as administrator for the Children's Bureau, my father made recommendations regarding the disposition of where children were placed. Some of the children had been abandoned, abused, or neglected, just like his own children. Dad was the guardian of his stepsister, who had an intellectual disability. I believe that probably motivated him to do the type of work he did.

Outside the home, Dad was both knowledgeable and likable. But over time, his employers were enablers, because if his excessive drinking was visible and a problem to me, a child, it certainly was detectable to them.

If someone works in any capacity with children, and they have children of their own but don't appear to have a healthy relationship with them, that should be investigated further. We need people who are healthy and care about children to be in charge of their well-being. Healthy and unhealthy relationships with children tell a story, and we need to pay attention. Doing the right thing when it comes to people, our humanitarian responsibility, doesn't mean placing yourself in harm's way, but it does imply that you don't allow others to be. Call the proper

authorities and let them do their job. If you don't see that occurring, go over their heads. The media is another resource that has been known to substantially advocate for children.

For years, people from his job called, looking for Dad. He was supposed to be at work by 8:00 weekday mornings, but during the summer, I'd often watch him leave for work at 1:00 or 2:00 in the afternoon. I didn't know why Dad wasn't going into work on time, but eventually, I discovered the reason.

Since I played sports, the day after a game I'd look in the local newspapers—the *Greensburg Tribune-Review* and the *Latrobe Bulletin*—to see the write-up. One time, flipping through the papers, I caught something about my dad in the local section. The *Greensburg Tribune-Review*, which covered Westmoreland County, had a police blotter that included write-ups of people who'd gotten DUIs, so people in the community knew. There he was, for all to see. It was another massive red flag.

If a parent or an adult who is in charge of children has an alcohol or substance abuse problem, that should be investigated without the parents present.

Dad drove a long silver two-door Cadillac sedan with a dark-green leather top. When he came home at two or three in the morning, once in a while he'd be so drunk that he'd crash the car into the white garage door. When that happened,

I knew it was going to be a bad night. I was used to his rage and
drunken routine, so before he got home, I'd lock my bedroom
door when I went to bed.

Dad was a heavy smoker, and regardless of how often my
clothing was washed, it always reeked of Newport cigarettes or
cigars. In the mornings, the pungent stench of his cigarettes
was another indication that Dad was home. I'd go outside and
find the car parked at a forty-five-degree angle in our two-lane
driveway, indicating that he'd barely made it home. The garage
door would stay broken for a while, but the neighbors never
questioned what happened or said anything. He'd fix it, only to
break it again and again.

**If something with the home looks out of
place—fire damage or a car smashed into the
garage—or it appears neglected, question
whether the parents are in the house or are ill
and unable to take care of it. That is an indication that the children may be neglected, too.**

The upstairs area of our house was a relatively confined
space that held the disgusting odor of Dad's cigarettes and alcohol when he was home. Often, when Trish and I were getting ready for school in the morning, we'd find Dad, still in
his suit and tie, passed out on the hallway floor. Whenever he
was lying on the floor, we tried not to wake him, so we never
wanted to check to see whether he was dead or alive. We were
so used to seeing him in that state, it wasn't worth the risk of
upsetting him. We'd just step over his six-foot frame and go on
with our day. That was our normal.

I went days at a time not knowing when or if Dad was coming back. We would just get up and go to school on our own. On the days he was passed out and went to work late, I knew he wouldn't be home early.

Although Dad was still gone most of the time, he never deviated from his demand that the house be kept in perfect order—probably a holdover from his life in the military. Saturdays, my little sister and I weren't allowed to leave the house until we vacuumed, washed dishes and windows, scrubbed floors, polished the table with lemon Pledge, and did the laundry. It was all about appearances over substance.

Dad was handsome, lean, and clean shaven, and he worked out at the Latrobe Elks Club. Over time, though, his dark hair receded on both sides and his facial features changed. On Mother's Day, a year after Mom passed, Dad was out drinking until four in the morning. When he attempted to drive home drunk, his tires hit a curb, catapulting his car into the living room of someone's house in Latrobe, which made the front page of the newspapers. Choking on his blood, Dad came within seconds of dying. Had it not been for an emergency tracheotomy, he would have. But my father never went to jail, and I wasn't aware he was even prosecuted for it. Yet the accident made an impact on his appearance. He had crushed his face and lost his teeth. His jaw was shattered and wired shut, leaving it permanently misaligned. He also lost his sense of taste and smell.

After the accident, Dad spent months in the hospital. Although I was only fourteen, as far as I remember, no one came to check on us, but we were already used to taking care of ourselves. After a few years of taking care of Mom, once Dad was released from the hospital, we became responsible for taking care of him. He couldn't get around well, and he had a little hole in his wired jaw where he could fit a straw, so we made his shakes. After the accident, he looked on the outside like the monster I knew him to be.

If an adult is in an accident related to sub-stance abuse, an evaluation of the situation should be done to determine whether there are children in the home and whether they are safe. Just because a parent is in a prominent position doesn't mean they are tending to their children or have a healthy household.

I'd hoped the accident was traumatic enough to end his drinking and his abusive ways, but it wasn't. Dad continued on his path of intoxication, and continued to put us at risk. There weren't any smoke detectors in our house, so the role of fire prevention fell to us. When he was drunk, he would often put water or food in a pot, then go upstairs and pass out. On several occasions, the heavy smell of burning and smoke prompted me to race downstairs to the kitchen, where I'd snatch a smoldering pot from the stove. If I hadn't, our house might have burned down. The way Dad constantly ruined pots, I had to use some of the money I would steal from him to get new ones.

I never felt comfortable in our home. My receptors stayed up, and I lived in fear of being injured or trapped in a burning house. When I told Dad about another close call, he'd warn, "What goes on in this house stays in this house!" I was terrified to tell anyone.

What happened to me as a child still happens to children today. To protect themselves, parents tell their children that their family's business is private. This veil of secrecy, where children learn to keep what happens at home quiet, predisposes them to harm.

We have to encourage children to be open to talking about things that don't feel right, both inside and outside the home. When something happens to children that doesn't feel right, they don't look right. Their behavior, patterns, and emotional behavior can all change. We need to encourage them to feel safe enough to talk about what's going on. If they can't trust the adults in their home, they won't easily trust you. Sometimes it takes work to help them. Do the work.

We would threaten to run away, but Dad would point and casually state, "There's the door." When we didn't leave, he'd add, "You're lucky to have a roof over your head." In time, I believed he was right, because we didn't have anywhere else to go. I felt homeless within a home. "Get used to it," Dad would say. He was the parent, and I was the child without a voice. His behaviors became customary and I was forced to adapt.

My mom's passing had triggered an avalanche of abuse, much of it aimed at me. After all, I was a reminder that his family had kept him from getting to the highest levels in the army. With our windows and screen door open in the summer, all that yelling and screaming should have caused the neighbors to be concerned, but no one ever asked if we were okay.

If you hear concerning sounds coming from a home, especially a home with children, if you aren't comfortable checking to ensure everything is okay, send the authorities to do a wellness checkup or call social services to check on the children. It is always better to be wrong than to allow children to suffer.

Dad's verbal attacks on me became so intense that Trish actually started to record them with a tape recorder because no one would have believed it. I was routinely berated and told I was "a loser," "a wimp," "a nobody," and that I'd "never amount to anything." He always said it so vehemently that I knew he believed it. Hearing my father constantly call me a loser stayed with me the most. Trish threatened to report Dad if he didn't stop, but that didn't matter to him. He laughed and said, "I'll tell them that *you're* the cause of this! *You'll* be the one in trouble!"

I couldn't believe my baby sister was trying to help me. When she played back the part of one recording where he called me a "pathetic, fucking loser that will never amount to anything," it ripped through me and settled in my soul. Dad could be so unbelievably cruel; we wanted evidence of his hateful behavior. But once we had it, we were too afraid to share it. We had become part of the code of silence. We knew we didn't stand a chance against a military hero and county politician. The risk was greater than any potential reward, and we knew it couldn't end well.

7

By high school, things were no better. Dad had no regard for us or our well-being. I remember I had one pair of brown lace-up leather boots that I wore all the time. Kids called me "Boots Claypool," and I carried that nickname until I graduated. It was another red flag that went unnoticed.

I didn't bother to explain that other than an old pair of tennis shoes I wore for sports, that pair of boots was all I had. I wasn't going to tell people we didn't have money for food or clothing because my dad was an alcoholic who didn't care about us. That my mom was dead, and we didn't have any other relatives around to look after us. Since Colleen was no longer in the house, we were literally raising ourselves.

I didn't feel sorry for myself, because I was functioning in survival mode. I didn't have a lot of time to reflect on myself or how I felt about everything that was happening. Instead, I was like a hamster on a wheel, each day focusing on the basics, like how I would get to school that day or how I would get food to eat.

I had grown up going to church, and in many ways, that helped me through. I didn't have a clear concept of my faith or a defined relationship with God, but the idea that there must be a purpose in what I was going through stuck with me. From time to time, I doubted my faith. But still, there was a vision inside me that kept me moving forward—a vision that some-day I would be telling my story in a book, and it would be a story of triumph. A story that would inspire others, about how I'd made it through and had done something meaningful with my life.

I'd put a smile on my face and go through each day, but I was often hungry. Really hungry. There was never much at home that my sister or I could make to eat for ourselves. Dad kept his steaks in the freezer in the small laundry room, mak-ing a mental note of how many steaks there were. If we ate one, he'd chastise us.

Retiring from the army left Dad lifetime access to the commissary at the army base. Every month, he'd make the two-hour round trip to a suburb of Pittsburgh. Occasionally, he took us along, but the food was mainly for him. Once in a while, on a Sunday, Dad cooked for us, but we were on our own for the rest of the week. His first few years in the army, Dad was a cook, so there didn't seem to be anything he didn't know how to make. On Sundays, he'd make steaks, homemade per-ogies, potato pancakes, or pasta with different sauces. During the week, if there wasn't anything for us to eat, I did what I had to do to survive.

When Dad would get so drunk that he'd pass out in the hall or on his bed, I'd slip my hand into the right-hand pocket of his sports jacket and slide out his gold money clip with his initials, CWC, engraved on it. My sister was terrified. Afraid that he'd kill me if he caught me, Trish would stand by the front door crying and ready to run if he woke up.

Although the amount of cash Dad had in his clip was never scant, I was always careful not to take more than two or three twenty-dollar bills because Dad was a master of tracking down his money when he sobered up. We knew that when he woke up, he'd count his money and figure it out. When he asked about his money, I'd say, "I don't know what you're talking about." He could hardly argue in his defense when he was hungover. For all he knew, he could have wasted the money he thought was missing at the bar.

I'd take just enough money for us to eat for a while. Usually, I bought the basics—milk, bread, eggs, oatmeal, snacks to eat in between meals, peanut butter, jelly, and orange juice. The cashier would put the groceries in big brown paper bags, and Trish and I would walk a mile and a half back home.

When children look malnourished or otherwise unhealthy, that could be a sign of significant issues. And if a child looks hungry or has to steal to eat, there's a problem. If a child looks like they're taking on responsibilities usually done by an adult, or has otherwise been put in a position to have to fend for themselves, something is likely not right. Any of these red flags should be brought to the attention of a guidance counselor, school nurse, principal, social services worker, or another authority.

Unhealthy behaviors in the home often bleed into other environments. Be cautious if a child is acting out of the norm or not up to par for their developmental age. A teacher can be a frontline advocate—noticing if a child is not doing homework, is stressed, stutters because

of stress, is malnourished, has poor hygiene, etc.—because they spend a significant amount of time with children.

Still, there were some bright spots. Just like I'd hang out at the lanes to bowl when I was younger, as I got older, I found a refuge in sports and in a special friendship that I credit with saving my life. Mark Burkhardt was one year older, and we bonded over our love of sports. We would play baseball together, and softball in Saint Vincent's league.

When we played, it was like we were in another world. Saint Vincent's sports programs were hugely popular in the town, and as the team's starting shortstop and leadoff hitter, I often appeared in the local paper. People would recognize me at the grocery store, and I felt like a celebrity. And sometimes I got to hang out with real celebrities.

When the Pittsburgh Steelers were in town for training camp, it was like Christmas in July. We shared the same locker room, and it was inspiring to see these guys and watch their scrimmages. When we had games, it wasn't uncommon to see some of the Steelers sitting up on the hill, watching. It was more than my father ever did. He never followed any of the sports I played or attended a single game. He relentlessly called me a loser. As much as I tried not to show it, it hurt. I was insecure and harbored self-doubt. However, being the star shortstop and having my achievements with softball and basketball written up in the paper gave me a lifeline.

Some days, Mark and I would have a softball game followed by a basketball game. We'd finish the softball game, then change our gear and head straight downtown to our basketball game. When we played in both leagues on the same night, I'd often be written up in two different articles, which helped neutralize the war within me regarding my self-doubt. It put something back that Dad kept working to take away. I threw right-handed, batted left-handed, and hardly anything got by me. I hit doubles and had quite a few home runs, but there was no sense in looking in the stands for anyone to cheer me on. Some parents have to miss their children's extracurricular activities because of work. I understood that. It was just that everything I did seemed to be such a big disappointment or of no interest to Dad. I just thought that it would have been nice to see him once. Maybe it would have changed the way he viewed me, and he'd stop calling me a loser.

That was another red flag that something was wrong at home.

While it isn't always possible for parents to attend their children's sporting events or extracurricular activities, it isn't normal for coaches, teachers, or those responsible for their children to not meet, ever see, or at least talk to the parent over the phone. If a parent doesn't demonstrate any interest in their children, that could indicate a fracture in the relationship or a problem in the home. Extracurricular activities are a way for children to showcase their talents to the people closest to them. Children want their parents to take pride in them. If you're a teacher, coach, or parent of another child participating in an activity and don't see this occurring, do not dismiss this.

I wanted Dad to find something about me that he was proud of. But while that wasn't to be, sports gave me a healthier sense of identity and helped fend off the destruction that came from my father. They kept me off the streets and off drugs.

In time, I took pride in knowing that I could accomplish things without his support. Seeing how hard the Steelers worked, and interacting with them from time to time, gave me hope. I saw a different way things could be. It made me gritty and determined, and that's still with me today.

Plus, there was Mark, whose energy and enthusiasm helped keep me afloat. Even though Mark and I were close in age, he was more than just a best friend—he was a mentor. He cared about me. I looked up to him, and hanging out together saved me from getting into trouble. As teens, thanks to Mark's influence, we started to reach out and mentor younger kids at Adelphoi Village—the local organization my mom had helped run, for kids who'd been abandoned. It gave me a sense of agency and hope. I was making a meaningful commitment, and I had Mark to thank for it.

To this day, Mark remains a close friend of mine. He still lives in Latrobe, and not surprisingly, he's a public servant, working as an elected official for Westmoreland County. We can all be someone's Mark—that one caring person who makes the effort to reach out and connect with someone who's struggling. It doesn't take much. Just offering a kid some kindness and attention, helping them to feel seen and like they matter, can make a world of difference. It may even save their life.

In many ways, my early experience mentoring kids was a continuation of my mom's work. Like Mark, and in many ways my father, before she became ill, Mom was very active in our community. Unfortunately, I never got to know my mom that well, but I knew she innately cared about people. She helped to fundraise for and run a treatment center for at-risk youth, the Adelphoi Village. She did this at the beginning of her second battle with breast cancer, so it was evident that her love and care for children eclipsed her concern for herself. She went on to start halfway homes for children who were abandoned or abused. She never stopped until the cancer stopped her.

My mother was always passionate about children. She didn't just say it, she went out and proved it by helping to raise money to build a playground not far from our home. She wanted children to have a safe place to go and have fun. Home isn't always fun—or a safe place for children. I know because the playground was the epicenter of town, and it helped save me. Rather than indulging in the drugs and alcohol that penetrated our community, I spent the majority of my free time there when I wasn't bowling and before I got into organized sports. It was my haven when home wasn't. I don't believe I'd be alive today if not for having access to that playground and basketball court. Somehow, after Mom's passing, her imprint remained at that park, and it was my connection to her. It had basketball courts, monkey bars, swing sets, and a merry-go-round. Mom believed it was essential to have safe places for children, but when she helped build it, I wondered if she had her own children in mind.

Mom was always doing something to help others in her way, and I felt that I needed to do the same in my own way, and she was a great role model. The example Mom set made me want to put in the effort to be a productive person and help people. She didn't want anything in return other than for children to have a better chance at life. I never knew if there was more to her story that was a driving factor. But that really didn't matter. She gave what she felt was a necessary contribution.

Find ways to invest in your community and care about the people in it, whether through your

profession or in some other way. That's important. Providing safe spaces within a community—places where kids can get food and shelter, or even just play—is one way we can support children who are being abused. Also, when you see a child who spends more time at the playground, or the local basketball court or track, than at home, that's an indicator that something might be wrong. When children need a safe place to go, or when they display chronic or significant anxiety, ask why. You can engage the child in conversation to see if they might offer any clues as to their situation at home, or raise a flag with another community-involved person or agency to keep an eye on them. Even just befriending a child sends the message that there's an adult who cares about them, and that can make a huge impact on their self-esteem.

I couldn't afford to attend summer camp for basketball or baseball, which placed me at somewhat of a disadvantage because the other kids participated in those camps. Since I couldn't afford it, I started working. Work got me out of the house and allowed me to buy food and clothing, so I enjoyed it. I only spent money on necessities. I thought anything else would be a waste. In some ways, I think that was preparing me for what was to come.

It's great for children to learn the value of money, but having to work to buy their own clothing, food, and other personal things should be concerning and warrants investigation.

From day one, it seemed I was at a disadvantage since Dad had so much animosity toward me and I couldn't control how he felt about me. Whether a child admits it or not, they want their parents' love. They want to feel safe and protected. Whatever makes them who they are largely stems from their childhood and life experiences. My upbringing caused me to think I was scrambling to catch up with the rest of the world—although I didn't know what the rest of the world was like. Because I had no one to guide me, there was a lot I had to figure out on my own without knowing if I was taking the proper steps or making good decisions. Regardless, I always tried to do the right thing. Although I didn't realize it at the time, working was helping to build my character and making me more independent. I didn't know what other children were going through, but I focused on doing my best. That's all I could do. The alternative was to give up, and for me, that wasn't an option. I had to see what was on the other side.

At sixteen, I worked at Super Burger for a year, flipping burgers and making fries. Then, when I was a junior in high school, I started working at the Latrobe Country Club as a caddie. When Arnold Palmer had private parties there, I, along with my buddies Mike Ferguson and Keith Flodin, would park cars for him. Working was part of my emotional escape.

8

When I graduated from Latrobe High School, I decided to apply for college. At that point, I really didn't have a sense of self. All the messages I'd heard from my dad were negative and toxic, and as a result, I didn't know who I was. But there was one thing I knew for certain—I wanted to be a trial lawyer.

I came to that decision in the fifth grade when I went over to my buddy Mike Ferguson's house after school. Mike's dad, Richmond Ferguson, came home from work wearing a nice dark-blue three-piece suit and tie, carrying a black briefcase. I asked Mike what his father did, and he told me he was a lawyer. As I learned more about his father's profession, it piqued my interest. Our teacher had given us the assignment of doing a career paper, and I selected "lawyer" as my profession.

I applied to Penn State University, even though I didn't have the best grades. Through a series of letters, I attempted to convince the admissions staff of my passion, drive, and ability. It was my first attempt at stating my case—something I'd do over and over again in my future career. Fortunately, it worked, and I was accepted. My plan was to major in political science and minor in business administration.

Both my parents had served our country courageously, and I was proud of them for that. Most assumed I'd take that path as well, especially after my brother joined the military out of high school. When I told Dad I wasn't joining ROTC or going into the military, he became even more inflamed, insisting that yes, I *was* going into the army. "No, I'm not," I told him. "I got into Penn State."

After I voiced my intent not to pursue anything military related, Dad threw all my clothes and belongings on the front lawn. At the very least, neighbors should have seen that as an indication that there was something dysfunctional occurring in our house. But no one asked what happened.

When tragic events occur, it's unbelievable how many people say they knew or suspected something was wrong. Call the child abuse hotline if you see a parent throw a child's belongings in the front yard or out of the house.

I struggled during my first year. Like lots of kids who've grown up with abuse, I wasn't prepared to focus. I took a lot of history with me, which made the transition from home to college challenging. I was a C student in my freshman year, and honestly didn't think I'd make it. I had left the house, but the house hadn't left me, plus I couldn't help but worry about Trish.

Also, I knew Dad was waiting to see me fall on my face. He was still upset that I hadn't joined the military as he'd wanted, and as my older brother, Charles, had. I realized that if I failed at school, I would be giving Dad what he wanted, so I pushed myself harder. Unfortunately, every time I went home, Dad was ready and waiting to try to undo any gains I'd made in terms of my self-esteem and self-worth.

One winter break, when I'd returned home for a visit, Charles stopped by. He was physically fit, with the physique of a wrestler, while I was very thin with no muscle definition. When I had started sprouting in grade school, I stood so frail that some children called me "toothpick" and "fuzz head." Even in college, I was thin, appearing malnourished because I was for a good part of my childhood.

Living in Lawson Heights had been tough; it was a blue-collar upbringing. When I was younger, my brother protected me on occasion from bullies. We would meet the bullies behind the Lawson Heights shopping center to fistfight.

Watching Charles fight on my behalf helped me gain the courage in high school to fight on my own, which I did, garnering some respect and honor in Lawson Heights and Latrobe. Fighting became a way of survival. I got into several significant fights simply because I didn't fit in. I was an athlete, but also a bit of a nerd. In that town, drinking and drugs were becoming widespread, and it seemed you were on one side of it or the other. If you were on the other, you weren't necessarily popular.

Ironically, while Charles had been my sometime protector from bullies when I was younger, he also held the same aggressive attitude, and as a result, I watched my step around him, trying to avoid any kind of confrontation. As with my dad, to some extent I can sympathize with my brother's behavior. He wasn't a bad guy. He was wrapped up in the same cycle of abuse and trauma that I was, and that my dad had endured. Charles and I were different people, and we reacted to the situation differently. That's common among siblings in the same household—how one handles trauma can be very different from another. You figure out any way you can to survive.

Late one evening, Charles and my dad were in the living room drinking and commiserating over military stories. I was a seventeen-year-old freshman at Penn State University and not part of their culture, so I knew things could go south really fast.

When Dad was drunk, he started calling me "big man on campus" in a belligerent manner. Words are as lethal as physical violence and powerful enough to kill, and I didn't want any part of their negative energy that night—it felt bad. Their voices escalated as they berated me in an attempt to lure me in, baiting me to defend myself. I didn't. I had grown tired of the toxicity, but I didn't have any other recourse at the time. I'd been wounded enough to see the brewing tension as a warning. So, I retreated to my bedroom, locked the door, curled up in a fetal position on my bed, and hoped it would pass.

The commotion downstairs was so loud it was nauseating. As the volume rose, I became certain it would manifest into an outburst of rage, and I was right. Only a few minutes after I left, there was pounding on my bedroom door. There are moments when you cannot adequately describe fear, and this was one of them. I felt trapped, and that night, I didn't think I was going to make it out of there alive. I prayed, then slowly opened the door, climbed back in bed, and assumed the fetal position, hoping to de-escalate the situation. Dad flew into a belligerent rant. His voice was powerful. When he spoke, he commanded attention, and for us to do what he ordered. You didn't challenge my dad. Even when I wanted to, I just didn't, because I knew better. His nickname was the Major because that's who he was, through and through.

"Who do you think you're betraying? You're a loser, coward, and traitor! *This country!* I fought for this country! I was in bomb disposal! I detonated bombs!" he yelled.

Yes, my father was incredibly brave, and he might have helped many others throughout his military career. But his

measure of being a man was war—fighting for our country—
and nothing else. One wrong move and Dad would have been
blown to shreds, just like those bombs he used to defuse. I admired his fearlessness; that takes courage and dedication. But I
wasn't like him. And I didn't want to be, because I didn't want
to be that type of parent. As tough and aggressive as my father
was, my mom was the toughest of all of us. A former marine
who fought a war against a cancer we knew nothing about,
twice. Plus she was loving and compassionate. I wanted to be
courageous and care about people and kids the way Mom did.

"You are a pussy! Who do you think you are, not doing
ROTC?" Dad roared, throwing his hands in the air. "You're a
nobody! You're a fucking loser," he continued, his voice filled
with disgust, void of empathy. He didn't care where his words
cut; he just made sure they sliced deep. At that moment, I realized my father had mastered the ability to make me feel inept.
I wasn't able to defend myself against a war hero, and it would
have been insane to try. I would only have given him a reason
for this to escalate into something I was unable to handle. I
smelled the alcohol, so I knew it was pointless for me to respond. Still, it hurt. I was a productive person, doing something with my life. I was working, going to school, and staying
out of trouble—I didn't know why he was attacking me and
why he hated me so much.

I wasn't a nobody, and no one would want to feel as if they
were nothing. Dad had never finished high school, and he had
a good job. Maybe that's why formal education wasn't high on
his list of priorities—he didn't see the value in it. According to
him, it shouldn't have been on my list of priorities either.

I took the criticism until I realized that if I didn't stand up
for myself, it wasn't going to stop. As amped up as he was, this
could go on all night. So, I asked if I could leave the room, but
my father and brother stood next to each other, blocking the
door. I couldn't get out, so I stayed in bed. Dad wanted to see

me break mentally and emotionally. Finally, I started yelling back, "I'm not a loser! You're fucking pissed because I want to make something of my life! You're pissed because you didn't do the things you wanted, and I am! I'm going on a different path! Not yours!"

And cut! I'd just given Dad what he wanted. He knew how to bait me, and he'd gotten what he needed. He turned around and walked away for a minute, but my brother didn't leave. My stomach tensed so tightly that it hurt my whole body. I knew I'd messed up. I curled into a ball, expecting the worst. When Dad returned, he had a revolver in his hand. Then everything seemed to happen in slow motion, but his words were fast. He yelled at me with a level of rage I'd never heard. As though I had mentally muted him, my mind didn't take in a single word for the next sixty seconds. I tightened my fetal position, my hands shielding my head. When my father pressed the barrel of his gun to my left temple, the mute went off. The fear and alarm in my brother's eyes amplified mine, and I closed my eyes.

"You think you're going to tell me what you're going to do after all these wars! I'll show you!"

Tired of being scared to death, I was ready to die if this was how it would happen. At seventeen years old, I was exhausted.

I inhaled deeply, believing it was my last breath of life.

"How does it feel now?" he taunted.

I didn't respond. My body trembled and my eyes watered, but I didn't cry out or beg for my life. If I had, it would have validated his disparaging remarks. How did *he* feel, pressing a gun against his son's temple for no reason other than his hatred for me? If that's what he needed to do to feel empowered, he was sick! I couldn't stop him, and I wasn't willing to give either of them the satisfaction of having my last words to my father be begging him not to kill me.

Dad didn't pull the trigger. Still, he succeeded in killing a part of me that night. The only parent I had left had shown me just how much he hated me. The cold metal against my head made me numb and left a permanent mental imprint. I can still feel it today.

I glanced over at my brother and saw his expression. Dad's extreme behavior had caught him off guard. I couldn't say for sure, but I believe my brother stopped Dad from pulling the trigger that night. As soon as they backed into the dark hallway, I locked my bedroom door, recoiled on my bed, and cried.

I don't know how my siblings felt or how they interpreted their experiences, but people can live in the same house, with the same parents, and have different perspectives. Their experiences and relationships with their parents or guardians can be different. But this—this was mine. And I wondered if any of the other homes were like ours. Even as the years passed, Dad's explicit reminders played in my head. "You are never to talk about any of this." The reality was that even before that night, on many occasions, my heavily intoxicated father could have intentionally or accidentally blown my brains out. Dad played an emotional game of Russian roulette that I'd never agreed to play. Either way, he won. If I wanted to survive, I had to bury that incident along with a trail of others. My reality was that other than my little sister, the only person I had was Dad.

9

After my freshman year, I put my focus and work ethic into gear and applied myself. For the first time in my life, I created a healthy routine. I'd been on pins and needles, navigating through land mines, since Mom died. Half my mind journeyed back to freshman orientation and the faculty's prediction of how many of us would flunk out during sophomore year, while the other half was embracing a defining moment. I had to get gritty and do the work.

Admittedly, I was a lost soul that first year, and I had to put some kind of manageable system in place. There were twenty-five thousand students at Penn State's main campus in State College, Pennsylvania. Only 10 to 15 percent of applicants got accepted to the main campus for all four years. This was a big opportunity. It would have been easy to blame my childhood, drop out, and end up starting over. I was at a crossroads. Either I'd buckle down at Penn State or I'd never escape Latrobe, Pennsylvania—the place of all the trauma.

So, for the first time in my life, I built a structure. I scheduled my classes to end at 3:30, which allowed me to play basketball. I had considered trying to join Penn State's baseball team as a walk-on and inquired about what it would take, but I found out it was a yearlong process with intense training. I thought the demand on my schedule would be too hectic, and I didn't know how to multitask at that point, so I let the idea go. I fed my appetite playing basketball with some of the guys on Penn State's team at Pollock Square on the university's campus. In the fall and spring, I'd show up and play a game, then hit the library until midnight. In the winter, during the week, I'd trek a mile up to the rec hall to play ball and lift weights. Basketball provided a therapeutic release; it was a lifeline the entire four years. I never drank or partied, so basketball balanced the pressure. We got our share of inclement weather, but nothing stopped me from going to rec hall and running a few games, hitting the weight room, then ending up in the library until midnight. And when I had the time, I hung out with my high school valet parking buddy Keith Flodin.

I also looked to another role model for inspiration. Joe Paterno had played football at Brown University. While he loved sports, he also believed in academics. He, too, had been enrolled in law school, but Penn State hired him as the assistant football coach before he graduated. In 1966, he became the head football coach at Penn State. When I started Penn State University, I'd often see Joe in the library with guys from the team. He was known to monitor the library to ensure no one else signed in his players.

Penn State wasn't just a football school. It appeared that Joe actually wanted his players to graduate. It was well known that if they didn't get the grades and weren't in that library, they weren't playing. As someone who could easily have spent most of his time playing sports, that inspired me to prioritize my studies.

Saturday was the only night I had to go out, but it was worth staying focused on my goals. I rallied during my sophomore year and ended up with a 3.8 GPA. By the end of school, I just missed graduating with a collective 3.6 GPA, but I became a member of the Golden Key National Honour Society. As it happened, our speaker at that event was Joe Paterno.

I graduated from Penn State University when I was twenty-one years old and applied to Villanova Law School, but I wasn't accepted. I was put on the wait list and told if I went to work for a few years, I could get in.

I took that recommendation and started applying for internships. In August, I entered the graduate economics program at American University in Washington, DC. Completing a twenty-hour internship, two days a week, was part of the program, and I didn't waste any time when I arrived. I walked around DC from one building to the next until I had holes in my shoes, begging anyone who'd listen for a chance to do an internship. I was thrilled when my efforts paid off and I became an intern for Senator John Heinz III at the Russell Senate Office Building.

Drew Forsyth was a legislative assistant for John Heinz, and he noticed I was lacking in the wardrobe department. He generously loaned me $350 to get a new suit and shoes.

After my internship, I started a paid position working for US Congressman John Murtha Jr. as a staff assistant. Although I was broke and barely had money for food, I decided to remain in DC until I got into Villanova. In the meantime, I survived on the free food served at the many lobbying events to which Senator Heinz and Congressman Murtha were invited.

10

That winter, after I'd moved to DC, I went to visit my older sister, Colleen, in Selinsgrove, Pennsylvania. I was driving back to DC on a two-lane road near Harrisburg. Suddenly, a car pulled out of a restaurant parking lot onto the highway in front of me. I veered to the right to miss hitting it, which sent my car crashing into the metal base of the restaurant sign. I didn't have my seat belt on, and I quickly learned a painful life lesson. The impact was so ferocious that my head slammed into the windshield. My lower lip was split open and left hanging below my chin, and a front tooth was knocked out. Blood covered everything. I was rushed to the local hospital, where I had to have reconstructive surgery to repair my lip. My face looked like a big purple balloon, and I was overcome with the most excruciating pain that wouldn't subside.

When I was released from the hospital, Colleen took me back to her house. My sister was kind enough to help me recover, but it was difficult. Dad never checked on me while I was in the hospital or while at Colleen's. Instead, he called a few days later and advised me that I needed to "get back to work.

You can't lose that job." Then he added, "It could be worse. You could have a brain tumor."

I didn't have a choice other than to manage without a tooth for a couple of months, but Dad was right; I had to get back to work. I couldn't lose my paying job with Congressman Murtha.

Between my physical discomfort and the years of emotional anguish I'd endured, my pain was unmitigated. I couldn't fix it, because it wasn't just one thing.

When I reflected on how little I meant to my father and realized how alone I was, for a moment I thought it would have been better had I been killed in that car accident. It didn't seem as though anything I did would ever make Dad accept or be proud of me. Drained, I didn't feel I had anything left to help push me forward, and I wondered if Mom felt that way at the end—like there was nothing worth fighting for that was worth all that pain. How do you overcome adversity when you're drowning in it?

Children can't easily separate themselves from unhealthy parents, but it helps when someone around them is tuned in to the fact that something is wrong. You can try to help get them the support they need to disconnect from toxic patterns and stop chasing the approval of abusive parents. Suicidal thoughts, or wishing for death, are a major red flag and a sign that that person needs help immediately. Seek support from a therapist or a suicide hotline.

When I returned to the house I shared in DC with two other guys who also worked for the congressman, I went straight into my bedroom, sat on the hardwood floor, and cried hysterically. That was one of my lowest and loneliest points. My gas tank was teetering on empty. I had an old mattress on the floor, box crates to hold my clothing, a folding chair, and a card table as a desk. What was I working so hard for? How would I find the energy to go on?

The dysfunction from my childhood weighed heavily on my soul, and I realized that it wouldn't disappear on its own. After flushing out that negative fear and emotion, the hysterical crying somehow refilled my tank.

Ultimately, I toughed it out and returned to work, even though my face looked like I'd just come out of a boxing match. In September, I finished my position with Congressman Murtha and once again started applying to law schools.

I was wait-listed at Villanova, my first choice, but I got into the University of Dayton Law School. I decided to enroll to stay on my path. I attended orientation at the University of Dayton, but on the last day, I saw a note on the bulletin board in the student lounge with my name on it. It read, "Call your dad. You got into Villanova." I was elated. I packed up my dilapidated Datsun 210 and drove ten hours, arriving at Villanova just in time to sign up for law school.

It seemed I was constantly being tested, but I believed there had to be a reason.

11

During my first year at Villanova, I worked in the bookstore on campus until I got a job at Bloomingdale's selling men's clothing. I learned a little about fashion and style while working the afternoon shift until the store closed each night.

After work, I went straight to the library to meet my friend Angelo MacDonald. We'd study until nearly 4:00 a.m., and I was grateful just to get three or four hours of sleep each night.

After leaving one such study session, when I got into my car and started it, the needle was below "E." I barely made it to the gas station on fumes, only to find my wallet was empty. I searched under my floor mats and on the ground around the pumps for pennies or whatever other change I could find just to get a single gallon of gas to get back home. Though I had a job and applied for every loan and grant possible, it wasn't enough. Between work and school, I was wearing myself down, and it showed.

During my first year of law school, my grades were less than impressive. I was in the bottom third of my class, causing me to feel ill prepared to compete in such an arena. But every one of my lessons prepared me for what was to come.

Colleen and her husband, Ed, provided a monthly stipend that I used in part to pay my housing expenses. Still, that first semester of my first year of law school, I barely had enough money to get by on, which meant I couldn't afford to purchase some of my books. I had to figure something out. I went to the library, copied the pages of the books I needed, and used them in class. One of my professors typically had students read aloud a description of the case we were about to discuss. One afternoon, he called on me. Noticing I was reading off papers, he asked, "Claypool, where are your books?"

Embarrassed, I said, "I don't have any books, but I read them in the library." He looked skeptical. "Let's give it a shot," I told him. "Ask me the question." It was humiliating, and I'm sure I looked irresponsible, but I managed to pull it off. With over a hundred students in that class, looking at me as I stood up for myself and my abilities, I was building self-acceptance and self-confidence. I was realizing that it was okay to be me, and to find creative solutions and other ways to get things done. That day in that classroom, in my exchange with my professor, I rose to the occasion. It became another defining moment in my life.

When I had a challenge, I told myself, *I can do this.* Everyone I had looked to in the past for support had told me what I couldn't do. As a C student, I was told I'd never work for a federal judge. *Never* is harsh—it's hopeless. It displays a complete lack of confidence. I had to expose that myth and remove the false label I'd been given by my dad, and by society, in order to become what I believed possible. In the process, it was my responsibility to gain what I was not given. It seemed I had been constantly trying to prove something to people who didn't care about me, and I wasn't buying into that system anymore. I started telling myself what I could accomplish. Perhaps that was my method of self-motivation, and it was beginning to work.

I didn't have a computer, so when it was time to apply for internships, I sat at my desk handwriting letters to federal United States Court of Appeals judges across the country. In an effort to be transparent, I explained how broke I was and how hard I'd work for them. Each letter was written with the belief that, somehow, I would defy the odds. I was relying on faith, but it was enough to encourage me to send more than forty letters asking for an opportunity.

I received one negative response after another, but I stayed motivated. All I needed was one favorable response.

One day, a letter arrived from the Eleventh Circuit Court of Appeals—Judge James C. Hill in Atlanta, Georgia. When I ripped open the envelope, the response read, "When can you come meet the judge?"

I scheduled the meeting to take place during the upcoming winter break. The day before the interview, my best buddy, Mark Burkhardt, drove me to the Greyhound bus station in downtown Pittsburgh to catch the overnight bus. I boarded the bus carrying a little plastic bag containing my razor, toothbrush, a comb and styling product for my hair, a sports jacket, and a tie. I couldn't afford to stay in a hotel overnight, so I didn't take anything else.

I sat by a window, watching the bus stop in what seemed like a hundred different places until we finally arrived at the bus station in Atlanta. It was 11:00 a.m. With just one hour until the interview, I rushed into the bus station bathroom, washed up, shaved, and did my hair. I walked outside the Greyhound station and asked a lady how far away I was from the US Circuit Court of Appeals. "If you take a cab, it's ten minutes," she replied. Oh no! I had planned everything except how to get from the bus station to the federal courthouse. I had a ten-dollar bill in my pocket to get something for lunch, and I hadn't eaten since I left. I couldn't take a cab. I had two feet and barely enough time, so I started sprinting. When I needed to catch my breath, I'd walk for a bit, then take off running again. I felt the adrenaline surge through me as though I were fleeing my father. I was running down a dream, literally, sprinting toward the goal of achieving that opportunity. I arrived at the courthouse ten minutes late, expecting I'd blown my chance. It was cold outside, but when I entered the office of Judge James C. Hill, I was sweating.

A petite older woman behind the desk looked me up and down and asked, "What happened to you?"

Nearly doubled over, trying to regain my breath, I explained, "I'm sorry. I—I know I look disheveled, but I couldn't afford a plane ticket. I took the bus from Pennsylvania."

"Oh my," she replied.

"Can you please convince Judge Hill to see me? Please," I begged.

She looked at me with the most understanding eyes and nodded at the chair behind me. "Have a seat," she said softly.

Ten minutes later, she came out of his office and said, "He's agreed to see you. You don't have a lot of time; make every moment count."

I nodded appreciatively and went into the office.

Judge Hill had been nominated by President Richard Nixon. His office resembled a law library. When I first saw Judge Hill, his thick gray hair and little round glasses resting on the tip of his nose reminded me of Santa Claus. Hanging on the wall behind him was a picture of President Reagan. He kindly invited me to have a seat. When I sat down, the back of the fancy leather chair extended above my head. I started to apologize for being late, but Judge Hill interrupted me. "Stop. I made an exception because you got here by bus. Now, tell me about your grades."

I was honest and told him I was a C student.

"Normally," he said, "I don't hire law clerks until after their second year, and definitely not if they are C students in the bottom third of their class."

Instantly I was demoralized. My father had told me I was a loser; I was not about to prove him right by losing this opportunity. I couldn't pack it up and become the failure Dad claimed I'd be. That would have been more damaging than not getting the job. I had to fight. Thinking quickly, I said, "If it helps, Judge Hill, there is a program that will pay half my salary, and you don't have to pay me anything. My grades are not as good as they should be. Not to sound as though I'm making excuses, but I worked in the bookstore and at Bloomingdale's to provide for myself and buy food. You can get your straight-A student next year, but sir, I am different."

"Tell me, how are you different?" he asked.

I didn't tell him about the challenges with my father. Instead, I told him about Mom and walking to deliver thirty-five newspapers in the deep snow in Latrobe, Pennsylvania. His countenance told me my paper route and my time at Super Burger weren't working, so I continued, "And I caddied at Latrobe Country Club."

Instantly, his eyes lit up and he sat up straight. "That's the home of Arnold Palmer," he declared.

When I'd caddied at the country club, I was grateful for the chance to be in such close proximity to a legend. I had no idea what role it could play in my future. At that moment, it all clicked.

"Yes, sir, it is," I said. I learned that Judge Hill was a diehard golfer who had followed Arnold Palmer for decades. Having grabbed his attention, I continued. "For several summers I worked as a caddy and parked cars for Arnold Palmer at his private parties. Let me tell you a story that taught me a lesson I'll never forget."

"Continue," he encouraged, giving me his full attention.

"One morning, I rode my bike three miles to get there, and I had the same ride home after my shift because my father taking me wasn't an option. I carried two golf bags for eighteen holes and was exhausted walking the hilly six-mile course. Including the tip, I made about twenty-five dollars. I was sitting in the caddy yard in the back of the clubhouse, where there was a bench and tables. The caddies usually hung out there until we were called to get a job. That day, I sat slumped over, completely beat, and I was the only guy in the yard. The caddy master came and asked if I was up for nine more holes. I said, 'No, sir. I'm sorry, I'm wiped out.' I rested for ten minutes. I grabbed a Coke, then hopped on my bike and started pedaling downhill on a meandering snakelike road. A couple of the fairways intersected with the road, and so I had to stop as a courtesy. When I looked over, I saw someone on the second tee—it was Arnold Palmer! My heart sank. That bike ride felt like it was the longest ride home ever. The next day, I found out for certain the bag I would have carried for the next nine holes belonged to Arnold Palmer. Sir, you can imagine how I reamed out that caddy master the next day."

Judge Hill chuckled.

"The caddy master told me that it was a lesson. And he was right. I never had another opportunity to caddy for Arnold Palmer, but I spoke to him a few times. The caddy master taught me that whenever you get an opportunity, you take it. That's why I'm here, sir."

I went on to tell Judge Hill about a time when Arnold and his wife, Winnie, were hosting one of their charitable events. My buddies Mike Ferguson and Keith Flodin and I flipped coins to determine who would park Arnie's car and open the passenger door for Winnie. I won the coin flip, so I opened Arnold's car door, shook his hand, and greeted him. Winnie was petite, five foot one and barely a hundred pounds, wearing a beautiful white dress and a neatly placed bonnet. Keith was on the passenger-side door. He was so nervous that he yanked the door open, the wind caught it, and it snapped back at Winnie, hitting her in the chest and knocking her back into the seat of the car.

Arnold was understandably upset. "How did you do this?" he exclaimed.

We stood in front of him stunned and devastated, not knowing what to say. We thought he was going to fire us on the spot. The three of us were almost in tears. Winnie took pity on us. She turned around, went over to Keith, and hugged him. "It's okay," she said softly. "You aren't going to get fired."

I watched Judge Hill's shoulders shake as he tried to contain his laughter. I wasn't sure whether I'd get the internship, but the interview definitely ended on a good note. It was no longer about my C average in law school, nor about being only a first-year student. Instead, it was about the heartfelt connection that Judge Hill and I made through storytelling.

With barely a two-hour window from the time I arrived to when I had to return, I was tight on time if I wanted to get something to eat before the long ride home. Judge Hill reached into his back pocket and took a twenty-dollar bill out of his black wallet. "Here. Take a cab," he said with a grin.

I took the money and thanked him.

When I walked out of the office, I winked at the lady who met me and said, "I made it count."

Thanks to Judge Hill's kindness, I made the two o'clock bus ride home.

Two weeks later, back at Villanova, I had just returned to the room I rented in an old Victorian home when I noticed a letter the landlady had placed on my dresser. When I tore it open, it said I was accepted for the internship. Judge Hill wrote, "The main reason I hired you was because of that story about Arnie," but he also confessed that he loved the diligence and tenacity I had displayed in getting there for the interview.

After my first year of law school, I packed up my beat-up Datsun and headed from Philadelphia to Atlanta. I had no idea where I'd stay when I got there, but I would figure it out. I had to. The first three days, I slept in my car. The little old Datsun had once been red, but now half of it was brown, covered in rust, with a gaping hole in the passenger-side door that wouldn't open anymore. If I took a girl on a date, she had to get in on the driver's side and climb over the stick shift.

I went to Georgia Tech and canvassed the bulletin board to see if there were any listings for housing close to the city. That was how I met Alan Cowart, whose dad, Robert, was the VP of Technical Operations at Delta Air Lines. Alan had a house that he rented to four other people, and he offered me one of the rooms. I asked if he'd allow me to pay rent two weeks later, when I got my first paycheck. The law school paid half my salary, and even though I told Judge Hill he didn't have to pay the other half, he did. Alan kindly accepted the arrangement, and I signed a month-to-month lease.

There was nothing other than an old mattress and a small wooden table in my room, but it was better than sleeping in my car. My first day there, I had gone to the store and bought two bags of M&M's—one plain and one peanut. In the middle of the night, I was awakened by a noise. Something was scuffling around in the dark. Then it sounded like something was in the little bag. I reached over to turn the light on and saw a big brown rat with beady eyes eating my M&M's. My screaming alarmed the other roommates, who came running in just as I jumped out the window. Over the next two weeks, I set traps in an attempt to catch that rat. While I was blessed to have always had a roof over my head, I was never comfortable. They weren't really homes but simply places to sleep.

I was late getting back to Villanova to start my second year of law school. I had committed to working for Judge Hill and

didn't want to leave early. I would be starting the semester behind, but what made the situation even worse was that a few
days before I returned to Philadelphia, someone broke into my
car by smashing the driver's side window. They sure picked the
wrong car, because the only things I had were some cassette
tapes and trash. I didn't have money to get the window fixed
so, being creative, I went to the store, bought four boxes of
Saran Wrap, and created a makeshift window, hoping it would
do the job until I could afford to have it replaced. A couple of
hours into my drive back to Philadelphia, the clouds grew dark
and heavy, signaling an approaching storm. I didn't know if
the Saran Wrap would hold, but I didn't have another option. I
was in North Carolina when that storm hit, ripping the plastic
off. Rain poured into my car, soaking me as I drove. People
started honking as they passed me by. I didn't know what to
do, so I just kept driving. If I stopped, the rain would have
just continued pouring in. It was stressful, and I didn't know
if I could handle much more that night. A couple more cars
passed me on the interstate, and one of the cars was packed
with a bunch of college-aged guys. The driver honked his horn,
and they looked at me and gave me a thumbs-up. Their simple
gesture empowered me to realize I could see it through, given
all the adversity I was facing. Maybe those guys understood
that. It's what I was learning to do at every level, and what I
was here to do with my life—see things through.

Still, there were times when I didn't think I would make it
through law school. Not having some of the books was humiliating, and I felt inferior to the rest of my classmates. Although
I kept doing my best, it always seemed as if I was one step
away from going in the opposite direction. Deep inside, I was
certain I'd regret quitting, and that fear of regret somehow
pushed me through the challenges law school brought. My father didn't believe I could handle adversity, and perhaps his
lack of confidence contributed to my not giving up. He'd given

me numerous negative labels, but although they hurt, I refused to accept them. He tried to break me in every way possible, and I couldn't let that happen. As much as I struggled, as low as I sometimes got, there was always a little more faith and fight in me. Some part of me knew this needed to stop being about my father. This was my journey, not his.

Again, I turned to sports to help me find a center point. For two of my three years at Villanova, on Friday nights I played guard in a graduate school travel hoops league. We played other graduate schools, such as Rutgers and the University of Pennsylvania. One of the guys on the team had a beat-up station wagon that the seven of us traveled in to get to the games. Several of the guys had played in college and fueled my passion. It gave me something to look forward to while eliminating the stress of just surviving. Feeding my competitive nature was fun and balanced the chaos. It helped me regenerate. I wasn't just surviving school—I was fighting to survive my childhood.

12

By my second year at Villanova, I was having a hard time justifying my visits home. Shuffling through my memories, all I saw was dysfunction, bad experiences, and remnants of Mom. Every time I elected to go home, I subjected myself to some form of abuse, as if I thought I somehow deserved it. After all, I knew what was going to happen.

I wrestled with the idea of returning, trying to discern whether home was truly the only place I had to go or if some subconscious part of me went back with the purpose of being revictimized. Perhaps it was the only way I got my father's attention. After all, that was what I sought, just not the way he gave it. It seemed as though I believed that what he gave me was better than nothing.

After graduating from Penn State, I had thought that when Dad saw that I didn't flunk out as he'd expected, there was a chance he would change his opinion of me. That he'd be proud of me for being man enough to take my own journey. In some strange way, despite his mistreatment of me, I was proud of what my dad had accomplished, and I wanted him to be proud of me. He was a war hero. Regardless of the abuse, that could never be negated. He had saved and led others. I wanted him to be that kind of person for me, too. I wanted to look up to him the way I'd heard others had. I was desperate for some form of affirmation, some indication that at some point, he would accept me. After all, I had done nothing to earn his hatred. What child could? Even if he had left the military early because of his family, he enjoyed a successful career as a civilian. Maybe he would get over his resentment. After all the emotional torture, I still loved him.

My second year at Villanova, I went home about half a dozen times, excited to see my buddies. The day before I went home, I'd call Dad and let him know I would be there on Friday at 4:00 p.m., to make sure he was there. One afternoon, I arrived after a three-hour drive to find that the doors were locked, and his car was gone. I called him at work, but he didn't answer. I knew where to find him. I made the thirty-minute drive to Mr. P's to find Dad sitting at the bar, drunk. Just like always, the heavy stench of cigarettes and alcohol wafted up my nostrils.

"There's my son!" Dad shouted when he saw me.

"Hi, Dad. The door's locked. I need the key."

He fumbled in his pocket, pulled out his keys, and removed one from the ring. Then, handing it to me, he announced, "My kid—he's killing it at Villanova." He raised his glass, took a sip, and continued, "He's—he's going to be a lawyer!"

Outraged by his fraud, I listened to Dad brag about me, though he vehemently condemned me behind closed doors. It was yet another way of reinforcing the code of silence. Bragging pushed away the idea that he was an unfit parent. It looked to others as if he supported me, like he'd played a role in getting me to that point, when he'd done exactly the opposite. At every turn, he had attempted to discourage me from pursuing my dream and force me to follow his. He'd tried to prevent me from having the confidence to think I could get to law school. Still, though it might seem obvious that it was time to let it all go and move forward without Dad in my life, it wasn't so simple. I grappled with what I should do. I'd never been able to gain my father's approval, and although I knew who he was and what he was like, I still had that yearning for his acceptance.

Christmas break during my second year of law school was the beginning of the end. The magnetic pull our enormously dysfunctional home had on me would finally begin to fade.

Our basketball team had won a pretty big game, and the newspaper did a nice write-up. Since I was mentioned in the article, I brought the clipping home and placed it on the refrigerator, secured by one of Mom's little fruit magnets. I hoped Dad would read it. I wanted him to be proud that I was managing both law school and basketball.

Walking upstairs to my bedroom, I ran into Charles. My brother and I didn't talk much, but my first day of break started off relatively normal. We went to the Greensburg YMCA to work out, then home. Nothing special, but nothing abnormal. He went about his day, and I went on with mine.

Just before midnight, I was in the living room watching a movie when behind me I heard the door slam shut. When I looked over my shoulder, I saw Dad, his face red and flushed. Each step he took was measured and firm, as though he had magnets on the bottom of his shoes. Suddenly, the room exploded with the same toxic energy I'd felt when he'd put his gun to my head and threatened to kill me. Charles came up from downstairs. I said good night to them and quietly slipped upstairs to my room, trying not to add fuel to the fire.

Apparently, Dad and Charles had seen my basketball article. They made their way upstairs and stopped right outside my bedroom door, where I could hear them joking and laughing about it.

"He thinks he's better than us. He's a traitor!" Dad shouted.

"He's not helping our country! But here he is again! Big man on campus!"

Frustrated that nothing I did made him say anything good about me, I responded, "Can you guys please respect me and leave me alone? I'm not bothering you—I'm on a break."

I had barely finished the sentence when my bedroom door slammed open, crashing against the closet door.

"Where are you staying for your break?" Dad asked, pointing at me. "This is *my* house! If you think you're the big man on campus—my other son's in the military," he said, patting Charles on the back. "I want you two to go fight in the front yard. Let's see who is stronger."

I had no desire to fight my brother. We were getting along just fine. I looked at my father in complete disbelief and asked him, "What are we fighting about?"

Dad didn't answer, but stood there looking as if the idea of my brother beating me up sounded like great entertainment. Even though Charles and I had no argument with one another, glancing at my brother, I could tell he didn't think he had a choice. It seemed Charles had to follow the military allegiance and comply.

"Let's go!" Dad demanded as if he were ordering his infantry in the army.

I couldn't believe I had willingly gone back to that dysfunctional place. It wasn't home. It felt more like a dungeon or a prison.

Reluctantly, I got out of bed and headed for the closet to get my shoes. After all, there were several inches of packed snow on the ground. "Now!" Dad shouted before I could grab them.

Barefoot, wearing plaid pajama pants and a Villanova sweatshirt, I followed Charles downstairs and outside. My brother was stocky, about five foot nine, and had a wrestler's physique. Knowing Charles was always prepared for a fight intimidated me. In the past, I had been forced to defend myself in several fistfights, so I had enough confidence that I figured I could at least protect myself, but that thought didn't last long. The moment my feet hit the cold cement patio, Charles cold-cocked me on the right side of my face, just beneath my eye. The hit was so hard that I fell flat on my back in the snow. Before I could get my bearings, Charles jumped on me like I was the enemy and shoved his thumb against my throat. Struggling to breathe, I tried turning my head away from my brother. Dad was standing there with his arms folded across his chest, a gratified smirk spread across his mouth. He was admiring my brother, pleased with his son's performance. Dad couldn't finish the job with his gun and blow my brains out, so he tried to manipulate my brother into doing his dirty work. Charles was the kind of child he wanted—one who did as he was told, without question. That was his way of handling what I have no doubt was a horrible experience for him as well. When you're faced with abuse, you just try to find a way to get through it.

Things began to go fuzzy, and I was convinced I was only seconds away from dying. Reaching up, I managed to scratch my brother's face. Reflexively, Charles reached up to cover his face, and when he let go, I flipped him off me and staggered to my feet. I ran out into the middle of the street, my frozen feet carrying me as fast as they could down the middle of the road, over a mile to Mark Burkhardt's house.

I pounded on their door, praying someone would answer. If they didn't, I had nowhere else to go. Fortunately, Mark's mom, who'd always been so kind to me, opened the door, and I collapsed inside. When I told her what happened, she took one look at my hands, then feet, and helped me defrost. I stayed with Mark and his family for the rest of my break. That was the last time I stayed at my father's house. I never blamed my brother for the fight, but I distanced myself.

**Parents should encourage healthy relation-
ships between children. If they do not, this is
a warning that something is not right. When a
parent pits one child against another, that is
a sign that something is mentally or emotionally wrong with the parent. If you see children
fighting, stop it, especially if you know a parent
is present. That is never healthy or acceptable.
Immediately contact a child abuse hotline.**

Finally, I made my decision—I wasn't going back to that dysfunctional house anymore. Once I made that choice, some of the things I'd struggled with started to become clear. I was going there because it was the only connection I had to a sense of family. The only place I belonged. But most importantly, that house was where I felt connected to Mom. I wasn't ready to leave behind that house, the chair she had held me in, and the old photos of her from before she became ill. Other than the park she'd helped build and Adelphoi Village, it was the only place where I could still feel her. But I had to make a choice. Even though it meant in some ways leaving my mother behind, I had to move on from the dysfunction, or the alcoholism, criticism, conflict, emotional and physical abuse, and repeated trauma would further damage me.

13

Between my second and third year of law school, I applied for and received an internship as a law clerk at a litigation firm in downtown San Diego. I packed up my Datsun, drove across the country, and worked there for four months. At the end of the internship, I drove three thousand miles back to Philadelphia, but at that point I knew that California was where I wanted to practice.

During my last semester of law school, I almost didn't graduate. I worked Tuesdays and Thursdays for a law firm in downtown Philadelphia to make money for necessities, taking the mainline train there and back. With all the time that ate up, it was difficult to impossible to make it to class those days. My last semester, the dean called me into his office and told me that if I missed one more Tuesday or Thursday class, I wouldn't graduate. He scribbled a phone number on a piece of paper and handed it to me.

"What's this?" I asked.

"It's a number for a local barber," he replied. "Go get your hair cut."

My hair was extremely long in the back, and admittedly, I

didn't fit the image of an attorney or a law student. But getting my hair cut wasn't a priority—I was focused on graduating law school.

Somehow, I squeaked by, attending enough classes to complete the semester. When I graduated, I packed a suitcase and flew to Los Angeles.

Completing law school is one thing, but the bar exam presents another challenge entirely. The test is grueling, and no matter how well you did in law school, hours and hours of studying are required if you want a real shot at passing. Preparing to take the bar was hard, but also exciting. It was a new journey—part of my new life.

A few weeks before the exam, I was studying in a room on UCLA's campus. I left for about forty-five minutes to get something to eat, and when I returned, all my study guides, notes, and books were gone. Everything! Desperate and dejected, I went to a pay phone and called Colleen because I was feeling like I wanted to give up. I'd already overcome so much to get to that point. How much more did I have to prove? How many hurdles would I have to overcome? The thought of being a loser loomed over me as if Dad were standing watch, just waiting for me to fail. Colleen encouraged me to keep going, and after I hung up with her, I walked back to UCLA and prayed about it. I had expected to have challenges, and now I needed to get through them without turning back and giving up. That drove me.

For some, their childhood or unhealthy relationships with their parents can make them want to give up. They may lack the confidence to succeed and overcome adversity. I certainly struggled with it. But knowing that I couldn't return home—that it was no longer an option for me—caused me to stop looking back. I had to create a future for myself instead of letting my past limit me. I had to figure it out.

As it ended up, I flunked the bar exam on my first try.

That's not uncommon, given how difficult the test is, but I had to keep my disappointment from derailing me.

I prayed about it and asked God for guidance on whether I should remain in California or go back to Pennsylvania. The answer was clear. I was tenacious and had a fighting instinct—ironically, something I'd gotten from my father. I'd dealt with setbacks before, and I could deal with this one. Most of my life had been spent fighting, and I could apply that aptitude to pass the bar. So for three months I isolated myself in a mobile home north of Pepperdine University and studied. On my second attempt, I passed.

Once the exam was over, I finally cleaned out my car. More than fifty empty Styrofoam cups, mostly from McDonald's, littered the passenger seat. My routine had been to wake up, grab a cup of coffee, and study. Those cups sure made a mess, but they served to remind me of my dedication. I had done it. Once again, I had applied myself and succeeded. Slowly but surely, my impostor syndrome was fading. I wasn't some loser who was getting by on luck. I was a capable person, able to apply myself and accomplish my goals. That might have seemed evident to someone else who'd just completed law school and passed the bar exam, but I had years of criticism and abuse to overcome—messages that had been deeply embedded in me. I would still have a long way to go, and in some ways, I still struggle with the things my father said to me, but it was finally starting to sink in. I really could do it. I really was achieving my dream of becoming a trial lawyer.

I had interviews scheduled with several firms in California, and one interviewer, Jacques Soiret, a senior partner at Kirtland & Packard, offered me a position as a defense trial lawyer. I accepted. The problem was that, once again, I had no place to live. (Professionally, I was good at looking ahead and planning. Personally, it was another story.) Fortunately, Jacques had friends in Westwood who let me live with them for six months, and I was able to take a bus to and from work. I offered to help around the house, run errands, and do land-scaping. To show my gratitude, I even ran errands for Jacques, too. I didn't mind, because I was living my dream.

As my new life unfolded and the pressure of school and the bar subsided, I began to reflect on myself. People have layers to them, and I was searching for the truth in this new layer. I didn't want to prove Dad right, so I became focused on winning as much as possible. I had no intention of going to a national firm to sit behind a desk for five years—I wanted to be on my feet in front of judges and juries, arguing cases. I wanted to become a great trial lawyer. So I dug in, working more than seventy hours a week and nearly every weekend. The cases were tough, and as it turned out, working on them took me full circle.

I didn't start out advocating for victims. I defended big corporations and government entities. I constructed a career, preparing to win every chance I had. You can't be the best trial lawyer unless you've prepared, and it was like learning a foreign language. I learned a completely new body of concepts that I'd never been exposed to before. For example, there are literally thousands of regulations in the Code of Civil Procedure. They are all the rules for all the courts, and you need to know them just to maneuver as a courtroom attorney. It's daunting. You have to know the uniform federal, state, county, and separate local rules of civil procedure. On top of that, specific courthouses within a county may have their own set of separate local rules that you have to comply with. The learning curve was brutal.

One of the most valuable insights I'd gleaned during my internship with Judge Hill was to not view clients as a numbers game. When I finished working for Judge Hill, he asked what I had learned, and naturally, I began reciting all these different laws. He raised his hand and shook his finger from side to side. Then he opened a drawer, pulled out a law book, and flipped through the pages, landing on one in particular. He said, "See that case, *Jones v. US*? Jones is a human being." He pointed at me and insisted, "Remember that."

Prior to that moment, I never thought a federal judge would be thinking about the litigants in his rulings in terms of their humanity—their hearts and souls. I thought a judge's job was to interpret federal law, and that's it. What Judge Hill taught me became the foundation of my entire career. *There are humans behind these cases.* It caused me to understand that I had to prepare thoroughly if I truly wanted to help people. When you see inside a courtroom day after day, it's evident that some attorneys are doing the bare minimum. I get it—caseloads can be massive. Instead of being overworked, others are just focused on the money. For me, it's not transactional or commodity driven—money has never motivated me. I'm driven to win, both for myself and my clients.

For the next ten years, I defended big businesses, eventually becoming a partner at Dongell Lawrence Finney Claypool. Our firm was on the fortieth floor of a downtown building overlooking the Hollywood sign. At our peak, we had twenty-five lawyers, and my name was on the door. I was doing what my father didn't think possible for me—I was winning.

I had all the outward signs of success—everything I thought would make my life perfect. But it wasn't. I'd created this courtroom persona, and while I was successful at arguing my cases, in some way, I had become a stranger to myself. Over time, as I continued to grow personally and become more self-aware, I realized that my soul wasn't satisfied. I became more and more certain that it was time for a change, but I didn't know what that would look like. Perhaps if I could make a difference in another way, I'd feel more fulfilled. I needed to discover my purpose, and how it tied into my childhood. I needed to do my work in a way that not only helped others, but in some way saved me in the process.

. . .

This shift in thinking was largely the result of the birth of my daughter, Alana. A few years after I moved out to California, I was at a happy hour in Long Beach, where I saw this woman with long, curly brown hair, wearing a purple dress. Something about her captivated me, and I struck up a conversation. Her name was Susan, and though at first I was drawn in by her looks, what hooked me was far deeper. As we talked, I discovered that she, too, was from a blue-collar town, and had used her scrappiness and tenacity to make a good life for herself and her young daughter. She was tough and committed to doing the best by her daughter. Her mother had also died when she was young. It was like we'd shared a common battle, one that immediately cemented an emotional connection between us.

Susan and I began dating, during which time she introduced me to a new kind of Christianity. I had been raised Catholic, but Susan was Protestant. It was very different from the church I'd grown up in, and I found in it a message that life was meant to be lived with purpose, to serve a higher calling. This church also felt kinder and more compassionate to me, which helped me become more vulnerable. I began to open up more and to start to see more clearly my faults and areas where I could improve. I saw something to aim for.

Susan and I were bonded, and I deeply respected and cared for her, but as it turned out, happily ever after was not meant to be. Over the next several years, we had an on-again, off-again relationship. We were engaged twice and called it off for various reasons. For me, one issue I just couldn't get past was that I wanted to have children together, and Susan didn't. She already had her daughter and didn't feel like she wanted to have another child with me.

Still, sometime in 2004, we gave it another try. As it turned out, Susan became pregnant, and we decided to make a real go of it. Alana was born in August 2005, and I was absolutely over the moon to become a father. I was completely in love with my little girl, but things with her mother weren't going as well. After about a year, we finally decided to go our separate ways. There was no way I was going to be an absentee father, so I fought for and won joint custody. I also helped Susan get set up in a house about forty minutes from LA, to make co-parenting easier for both of us.

Suddenly, I was a single dad. I took about six months off work so I could dedicate myself completely to my daughter. There were no nannies or babysitters—I changed every single diaper myself. I don't think I went on a date for four years, because I wanted to dedicate every minute I had to Alana. And I was delighted to do it. I was so happy spending time with my daughter and so grateful to be her dad that for about the first four or five years of her life, I kept a diary detailing all the things I loved about her. I would sit there at the coffee shop, with her playing next to me, jotting down notes to try to preserve every precious moment. I realized it was part of my mission in life to be a good father. I was going to break the cycle of trauma, and that meant being there for Alana in every way I could.

Prior to becoming a father, I had never spent much time thinking about the what-ifs or whys of life—I was focused on expanding my career and making partner. But now I was approaching that stage in life where I needed to know. I needed something deeper. I needed understanding and meaning. And I needed to help create a better world for my daughter. Caring for this helpless child made me realize just how dependent children are on us to protect them. Not just my daughter, but all children.

Also, I was increasingly aware that I needed to recognize and reconcile my past, and though I wasn't clear on how, I knew my work had something to do with it.

14

Sometimes change will happen on its own and force you to respond. Not long after I started to feel that it was time to transition into a way of working that was more beneficial to others, it happened. It wasn't the way I would have wanted it, but it was time.

Once, I thought Dongell Lawrence Finney Claypool would be the last place I'd ever work. That's probably why I was reluctant to make a change, even though I knew it was the right thing for me. But God also knew it was time.

My pastor, Jim Reeve, preached in a sermon about using your faith by weaving it into your vocation. At that point, I had just won eighteen jury trials in a row. When one side wins, the other loses, but I wasn't thinking about that. I could have been taking away from people by winning, but that didn't bother me. I was just doing my job.

Now, I wanted to see clearly what my mission should be and who I wanted to become. Then I realized that I knew—and oddly, I think I'd always known. I wanted to fight for those without a voice. I wanted to fight for kids, and for others who were disempowered within our systems. I knew what it was like to feel invisible and like no one was going to help you. I could change that for at least some people. I could stand up for them. I could amplify their voices so they could be heard.

I'd always had faith, but it was Pastor Jim who encouraged me to do something different with it—to integrate my faith with my work. He said, "Write on a piece of paper your Christian values, and try to bring those into whatever job you have." It was such a profound statement, and I was so struck by it that I took his advice. When I did that, I realized I needed to extricate myself from our law firm because I wasn't living the way I was supposed to be—in a way that aligned with my values—and I was fighting for what felt like the wrong reasons. Although I was successful in my career and brought in a lot of business, I wasn't happy. I was just trying to win cases. I was focused on the prestige of winning because I was still trying to erase the label my dad had given me. Children can spend a lifetime trying to undo the damage wrought by their parents and other adults.

One of my strongest and clearest values is being a good father. It's a priority for me to be consistently and meaningfully engaged in my daughter's life. One day, when my partners called wanting me to come to the office, I said, "I'm spending time with my little girl." I was the second-highest producer in the firm, and I put in a lot of hours, but I didn't want to be a dad in name only. I wanted to be an involved, loving, and caring parent. The next time they called telling me that I was needed in the office, I looked in the mirror, and asked myself some hard questions about my life and my work. I didn't like the answers, or the person I had to be at the firm, so I resigned my position. I left everything in my office and just walked away, knowing I'd never go back.

Financially, I was in good shape, but spiritually, I wasn't where God wanted me to be. I needed to protect and help people by doing something that positively impacted their lives—and I wasn't doing that. I hadn't had the childhood I'd had only to ignore the lessons or become an absentee father. I wanted to break the cycle. I wanted to take excellent care of my child, which meant being the best example possible—not only for others, but also for her. I knew I wasn't perfect, but I would do my best for Alana.

Somehow, I felt I had a bigger purpose. I wanted to be a better man, father, and child of God. When you truly begin to learn from your past, you will see the path you are supposed to take and the difference you can make.

After I resigned, I started handling cases working out of the den in my house. I was finally representing real people, individuals instead of corporations. It was just a few at first, but I quickly wished I'd made the transition sooner. This was what I was meant to be doing. It allowed me to be present and available for Alana while representing victims of civil rights violations. At first, they were smaller child advocacy cases. Not smaller in importance, to be sure, but smaller in size. Some were gunshot cases, where people had been unlawfully killed by police officers. Then I began to take on cases for children in Pasadena who had mental disabilities. Although they had individualized education plans (IEPs), their schools weren't honoring them, and I was able to help implement change.

At that point, life was a dichotomy. I was absolutely loving the experience of being with my daughter and working cases that had real meaning, but at the same time, switching gears had devastated me financially. I couldn't pay my bills, in part because I was fronting the expenses for my clients' cases. When you take on cases like I was, for families who have little or no money, you front all the expenses for them. The cost of investigations, expert witnesses, and depositions was all coming from my pocket. And the stakes are high. If you lose the case, you don't get paid, and you lose all the money you put into it.

At the time, I owned several properties in Arizona and

Nevada, and I started getting past-due notices on the mortgages. Then the short-sale notices started coming. I was losing everything I'd worked so hard to build. Still, to me, it was worth it. I was willing to put my resources on the line to fulfill my calling and to help people who needed me.

I told my pastor, Jim Reeve of Faith Community Church, that I was struggling with my path in life. He advised, "If you put your mission first, all the other things will come naturally, and you will be rewarded." I wasn't worried so much about being rewarded, I just wanted to be able to keep doing what I was doing. To keep fighting for others.

I became a warrior for children. It didn't really matter to me that I wasn't making any money; it felt right. My soul felt enriched and fulfilled. This type of work was saving me.

I started working for victims of sexual abuse largely due to Pastor Jim's sermon. I did what he said, and through my faith, I put my cause ahead of the fruits; the fruits would come later. Looking into my daughter's eyes helped me see the world differently. It wasn't about my name being engraved on a plaque in front of an office building. I looked at my life and career through a new lens, as a father and as a Christian. It gave me the strength of conviction to walk away from a base draw of $300,000 plus a bonus for the revenue I brought into the firm.

It was a bold move, and as it happened, I shifted the direction of my career just before the stock market crashed, which is what caused me to lose most of my savings and real estate properties. When I sought support from Pastor Jim, he said, "The tragedy will lead to trial. But if you stay true to a godly purpose, you will go down the road and see the benefits." I recommitted my life, sought positive spiritual affirmations to help me stay the course, and put God first. If you pay attention to your life, you will know when you're missing something. When you see it—even if you just glimpse it for a moment—it will move you.

Pastor Jim is one of the most influential people in my life, and I trusted him. I believed him when he said, "A setback is a setup for something much better."

It could have been a stressful time, but instead, it was liberating. I felt that I was finally letting go of a weight that had been on my shoulders. It's difficult for many to do, but it's possible. Staying part of that code of silence was starting to turn me into an ugly person. And I wasn't living with trust. When you cannot trust your parents, that can make it challenging to trust others, or it can cause you to be too trusting because you want what you didn't have. By the grace of God, my legal practice taught me. It helped me understand that the path I was going down wasn't where I had wanted to go. The cases I had worked for my law firm helped me become a better trial lawyer, but I realized that too often, I was on the wrong side.

I was a single dad, trying to do my best by my beautiful little girl, revamping my career, losing my properties, on the verge of losing my home, and my faith kept me from jumping ship. I was proud that I didn't put my circumstances above God's plan and abort the mission. When you begin to fight for what you believe in, if it's truly meaningful, you won't quit when you face personal or professional adversity. After all, lawyers are trained to face adversity—and win. There was no reason to fear taking the side that looked hopeless, because I knew how to fight. When I saw these victims and heard their trauma, the damage they'd suffered or the losses sustained, I realized they needed me.

I was finally on a path of recovery, redemption, and fulfillment. Part of my life was in turmoil with the financial challenges, but I trusted the journey. I trusted that God would take me to another place. I'd bought those properties and so many other things to prove that I was better than what Dad ever thought I'd be. It was my father's approval I had been seeking, when all along, it should have been God's. It took my find-ing myself at the bare bottom of the barrel to connect to and trust—*really* trust—God. Not when things were great again, but in that moment when I was struggling.

When you get to rock bottom, that pain will take you to the place you need to be, whether you know it or not. Pastor Jim always says, "If you are following the path of God, don't be afraid to pray for the fruits of your labor." I realized I could let my old lifestyle go and create a new one that centered on ful-filling my purpose. It dawned on me that life isn't about *living the dream* in the way we typically think of it, with all its mate-rial rewards. It's about living the most fulfilling and spiritually rewarding dream. You don't want to dream without faith.

Finally, I was on the right path. I knew where I was headed, I just needed to determine the best way to get from dream A to B.

PART III

SPEAKING FOR THE VOICELESS: LANDMARK CASES

15

I have shared my story to show how childhood trauma can affect a person's life. I do not mean to compare my experiences to those of the victims in the tragic and horrific cases I have taken on. The suffering and loss of life that the children from the following cases have endured is an unimaginable level of abuse. What follows includes horrific accounts of physical, mental, emotional, and sexual abuse, and murder.

You've already seen the degree of damage that the traumatic experiences from my childhood and Las Vegas have had on me. As you read on, imagine the suffering and trauma that will follow these children and others in similar situations. How these children have been stripped of a healthy, joyful childhood and a sense of safety, and how the experiences will impact them for the rest of their lives.

Perhaps this type of abuse is happening right now to someone you know. When we see any form of abuse, we are responsible for doing something about it. As in part II, I note a variety of red flags in the chapters that follow to help alert you to potential abuse, offer guidance for how to prevent it, and tell you what to do if you suspect that a child has been abused.

Our voice is the change and the most powerful tool we have to break the code of silence.

Before officially launching my new firm, I met with Pastor Jim, seeking reassurance about some of my decisions. Instead of advising me on what choices I should make, he spoke about the importance of fulfillment and how I might attain that feeling. What resonated with me most was his exhortation that it wasn't about the work I chose, but about adhering to my values as a Christian. He underscored that my primary goal should not be making money. That was easy. While I had enjoyed the fruits of my labor, money had never been the sole driving factor for me. What also resonated with me was the role I wanted to play in the lives of others. I wanted to not only serve those who'd been harmed but also be there fully for my family. I grew up with a father who was largely absent from home, and I wasn't willing to do the same to my daughter, whatever the larger motivation. That was nonnegotiable. My father was my template and gauge of what *not* to be.

Prior to speaking with my pastor, I felt I'd been on a treadmill, hyperfocused on proving to my father that I had intrinsic value. Finally, it was abundantly clear that I'd spent the majority of my life striving for an unattainable goal. But still, I was motivated to win—in life, for my daughter, and for my clients. Talking with Pastor Jim helped me align that focus with spiritual fulfillment. Winning now meant helping children. In that realignment, it became clear to me that my passion, which had been there from the beginning, would lead me to my destiny.

In contemplating all this, I also realized that helping children reminded me of my mother. I thought back to a plaque displayed in our home, symbolizing her dedication to children. It read, "In loving memory of Ramona Claypool, who tirelessly worked for the children of Lawson Heights." She always had an affinity for helping those who needed it most. Mom's life had been cut short, and I was reinvigorated by the potential of carrying on her legacy. I may have let her down for the first fifteen years of my legal career, but this was my moment to seize some of that opportunity back. I could honor my mother through my work—a realization that further validated my decision and made me want to get started as soon as possible. I was a decorated trial lawyer, and I would use my skill set to serve God better and help those who needed it.

When I left my salaried job, I no longer had a consistent income. Many of the cases I took were on a contingency basis, meaning I was paid only if I won. Having lost my investment properties in Arizona and Nevada, I relied on a single commercial property in Austin as my only regular source of income. Making a modest salary and losing things of material value didn't bother me. It was more important that I walk in my purpose. I had faith that a door would open elsewhere. If I remained devoted and focused on my daughter and on serving others, everything else would come when it was time. I was at peace with my decision.

One of my first cases was representing the family of a young Hispanic boy who had been shot in the head and killed by a police officer. To me, it was evident that the boy had been victimized and racially profiled, so I felt deeply compelled to take the case, even though I'd never handled one like it before. "If you bear with me," I told his family, "I will learn how to do this case." For me, this case marked the beginning of doing what truly mattered to me. But it also provided me with a difficult, if valuable, lesson.

During the course of the monthlong jury trial, I stayed in a rundown hotel, returning home on weekends. Our goal was to get the insurance company to pay $2.5 million to the family. Before the trial started, they offered a settlement of $1.5 million, but we rejected it. After closing arguments, there was a lunch break as the jury deliberated. On my way back to the

courtroom, the insurance agent pulled me aside and handed
me a letter. I went to Starbucks to read it. They were offering
the $2.5 million we'd hoped for. But I was so emotionally in-
vested in the case that my vision was skewed. I had put my
heart and soul into the case, and as a result, I had lost my
objectivity.

When I returned to the courtroom, I approached the father and told him about the offer. I asked what he wanted to
do. He asked if I would be okay losing, because what he really
wanted was a reckoning for the police officer. After a short discussion, we agreed that it wasn't about the money. We both
wanted the sheriff who had shot his son to stand up and face
the jury and their verdict. If we took the payout, neither this
cop nor the sheriff's department would learn. As it turned out,
it was a big mistake. We lost the verdict. In addition, I owed
nearly $100,000 in expenses. It was beyond devastating.

Once again, I struggled with my faith. Was I doing the
right thing? Was this really my calling? A few days later I
spoke to Pastor Jim. "There is a reason," he assured me. He
advised me to stay the course and said that if I stuck to God's
plan, I would get to where I wanted to be. Perhaps this experience would serve as motivation for me to do more to serve
others. He was right—it did motivate me. And later, I learned
that every great trial lawyer loses sometimes because they take
on the hardest cases.

So, I remained vigilant, patient, and dedicated to the cause,
and two years later, I had the opportunity to redeem myself. I
represented the mother of a twenty-year-old boy who'd been
shot by a police officer in Tulare County, California. We ended
up settling that case for $2 million.

As I learned, there are certain cases where the best course
of action is to settle, while there are others that must go to
trial. In those cases, a settlement likely won't bring about
what we are seeking—*change*. We want those involved to sit

through a verdict and understand the full effect their actions, or inactions, have had on the lives of the victim, their family, and their friends.

Though several of these cases were in some ways similar to the civil rights cases I'd taken on previously, there was still a learning curve. Most included children and people of color who had been shot by police officers, and I became somewhat of a champion of people who were being racially profiled. I was helping these victims' families, yet focusing on these types of cases helped me, as well, and when I needed it most. They made me feel like I had a purpose in the world and assured me that I was doing the right thing. Each time I got a new case, I saw my daughter's eyes in that child. At first, I thought winning was getting paid. Yet advocating for these children and giving them a voice also began to change me. It gave me something priceless—it nourished my soul.

Then came the case that thrust me into the spotlight. A civil rights activist connected me with a woman who claimed that her daughter had been sexually abused by a teacher at Miramonte Elementary School in the Los Angeles Unified School District. It was my first sexual abuse case.

One of the reasons I ended up focusing on these cases was my own childhood trauma. As a kid, I wasn't brave enough to report my father for his abuse; I didn't have confidence that anyone would believe me. If I reported it and the authorities or teachers felt I was lying or exaggerating, what would happen next? And what if they believed me? How would that affect my life? Would my father be notified? I couldn't risk either outcome. My whole life, I'd been haunted by my own silence. Now, I had a chance to be the voice for those who had none. If a child was too afraid to come forward on their own, when it came time to fight for them, I would be ready for battle.

We agreed to represent the young girl, along with eighteen more of the alleged victims from Miramonte. At the time, it was the largest child abuse case in history at a single school. The school system tried to buy our clients' silence. At the advice of their legal counsel, other victims opted to take the settlement. It was an understandable decision, as some were afraid of the consequences of drawing out the case any further. Yet I advised my clients to go to trial. I knew that an early settlement wouldn't bring about the change we sought. We needed a verdict from a jury.

I asked all the victims I represented to trust me and to allow my team to get them the justice they deserved. We wanted to figure out what had gone so terribly wrong that this abuse had been allowed to happen and to continue for so long. And we needed to know how we could keep it from happening again. Ultimately, that is what truly mattered—to create awareness and ensure social change moving forward. My clients agreed, and in a powerful statement, we declined the settlement. Then it was on to building a case.

Mark Berndt was a popular teacher. He was so beloved that, during his three-decade tenure at Miramonte Elementary School, he received invitations to many of his students' social gatherings and parties. But as is all too common, the abuser is often the last person you would suspect. Their status and reputation in the community tend to make people who do sense that something's wrong reluctant to speak up, and institutions are willing to cover up evidence of abuse rather than risk scandal.

One of Berndt's acts centered on a "tasting game" Berndt would play with his students at lunch in which he offered them cookies and asked if they wanted icing on them. As it turned out, the "icing" was his semen. It was horrifying, but true. Unfortunately, Berndt's history of abuse spanned decades. For years, Berndt plotted to get unfettered access to the children he victimized. One of his ploys involved sending notes to teachers supervising the lunchroom, requesting that students—usually two at a time—be sent to his classroom to help him clean and redecorate. Berndt routinely called for the kids in pairs to normalize his sexual predator behavior—the kids would think it was happening to both of them. The teachers allowed the kids to go to his classroom. After school was over, Berndt would stay on campus and send notes requesting that kids in the after-school program be sent to his classroom.

Insist on a consent form for the removal of a child from a class. If your school does not provide you with a consent form allowing your child to be removed from a class and sent to another classroom, this is a red flag. Do not consent for your child to ever be removed from a classroom other than for a medical emergency.

Be cautious when leaving your child in any after-school program. Insist on a written parental consent form to allow your child to go from the program to visit any teacher, regardless of their relationship.

If a child is asked to stay after class or extracurricular activities, this is a classic red flag. An authority figure may be developing an unhealthy connection to your child. Spending time with a child is significant, as children relish spending time with those they look up to. This can, over time, cause the child to drop their guard. As adults, especially parents, it's

our job to be aware of unusual connections between children and other adults.

As it turned out, the first claim filed against Berndt dated back to 1983, when a parent claimed that he dropped his pants in front of children during a field trip to the museum. School administrators placed notes in Berndt's file, but no other formal documentation about the incident was made. In 1994, a student accused Berndt of reaching for her private area during school. Once again, Berndt got off the hook when a prosecutor determined there was insufficient evidence to file charges or convict. After the Miramonte case, two students from the 1990s came forward and stated that Berndt would masturbate behind his desk during school hours. When they reported Berndt to a school counselor, the counselor told the two young girls to stop making up stories.

Were it not for a young woman at CVS Pharmacy, Mark Berndt might still be teaching and terrorizing children to this day. In 2010, a drugstore photo technician noticed that some of the pictures she was processing showed a young child blindfolded and gagged with clear tape. She contacted authorities, who, upon investigation, recovered nearly eight hundred photos with an eerily similar theme. Dozens of children with blindfolds and tape over their mouths in a classroom setting. Some photos showed children with cockroaches on parts of their bodies, or a spoon holding a white substance entering their mouths.

In the age of social media and smartphones with cameras built in, taking photos can easily

seem like no big deal. But be aware any time adults who are not those children's parents are taking photos of kids. What may seem innocent can actually be a lead-up to sexual predation. The adult could be using the pictures to satisfy lewd sexual desires, or as a mechanism to groom the children by telling them how beautiful they are, elevating their self-esteem. Pictures should never be taken of your child without your explicit consent. If you find this has happened, report it to the principal or a higher-up immediately.

Also, be on alert if a teacher gives children gifts. One girl who Berndt molested multiple times had a book that he had given her that included a handwritten note. When her mom finally searched her daughter's belongings, she found it. If a teacher gives a child a card, it increases the child's self-esteem, and then they like the teacher even more for making them feel "special." This behavior paves the way for disarming children.

While the photographs were damning, they alone were not enough to convict Berndt. We didn't have tangible physical evidence of abuse, and no witnesses from the school were willing to come forward. Some of the teachers were protecting Berndt.

Kids, teachers, and administrators loved him. It was as if he were invincible. Sexual abuse cases against school districts are often extremely difficult to prove because the organizations and schools are the gatekeepers of all the evidence. But fortunately, a detective from the LA County Sheriff's Department uncovered proof that was irrefutable.

When the LA County Sheriff's Department became involved, they began an official investigation of Berndt. Lead detective Marvin Jaramilla showed up at Miramonte unannounced to interview the teacher. Detective Jaramilla was leaving the school when, following a hunch, he decided to make a U-turn. He knew that Berndt would likely still be in the principal's office, so he raced to Berndt's classroom and checked the trash can.

Miraculously, Jaramilla found a spoon similar to the one in the photographs, along with a Tupperware container. Later, the LA County lab confirmed traces of semen on the spoon. The sheriff's department conducted surveillance on Berndt and through that process were able to retrieve an empty soda can. It contained his DNA, which matched the semen found on the spoon. It was an incredible moment for the investigation, yet Berndt could have been caught decades before if the school had taken seriously the claims that had been filed against him. If Detective Jaramilla had not followed his instincts and gone into that classroom, Berndt might still be abusing children today.

In 2013, he pleaded no contest to more than twenty counts of abuse and received a twenty-five-year sentence. Berndt would go to prison, but we also needed, and the victims deserved, for the school district to own up to their role in the continued abuse.

Some of the Miramonte families claimed they had told the school countless times about inappropriate situations involving their children and Berndt, but nothing was formally investigated. A game changer in the case came when we discovered that the school district had shredded hundreds of pages of reports documenting previously suspected child abuse. These are called suspected child abuse reports (SCARs). Sadly, organizations often try to hide evidence, making it extremely difficult to find the information you need. In some ways, taking these cases is like taking a leap of faith with God.

When we found out that the school had destroyed years of SCAR reports, we argued that the jury be instructed to infer that, based on the school district's actions, those reports contained information that would be adverse to the school. This was devastating for the school district and put the last nail in their coffin. In these types of sexual abuse cases, lawyers have to prove that the school or private organization "knew" or "should have known" about the child abuse. The destruction of the records proved that they knew. The fact of the children's molestation is not enough to win a civil case, but the SCAR can help you hold the school accountable.

After four years of fighting, we were ready to go to trial. The other attorneys and I walked into the huge courtroom where over a hundred potential jurors awaited the selection process. Some of us were picking the jury while two people from our team were in the back of the courtroom negotiating with the school district's attorneys.

When the case began, there were more than 150 victims, each of whom were offered $425,000 to settle. Roughly half took the offer, and in the end, a total of eighty-one students, victims aged eight to fifteen years old, officially accused Berndt of obscene acts. In addition to Berndt's conviction, the school district agreed to pay approximately $142 million worth of settlement claims. The settlement's size reflects the extent of harm imposed by the teacher, along with the school district's inaction surrounding the misconduct complaints that had been lodged against Berndt for years. The settlement was divided among the victims, who received nearly $2 million each, along with the three camps of attorneys who, along with their clients, stayed in the fight.

When trauma is inflicted upon children, it's irreparable. They can learn to manage it, but often, those recollections get buried until something triggers them and they resurface. When I fight for abused and neglected children, if they are awarded money, that doesn't release them from the pain, memories, and lifetime of trauma that comes with the abuse. Money doesn't bring about healing, but it is the driving component that brings about change. If you aren't involved in the case or otherwise know the darkest and most horrific details of what each victim suffered, it's impossible to understand what lawyers do for these clients and why. Every penny we get helps to punish the system that allowed a child to suffer or die.

If we had settled early and for a lesser amount, we would never have uncovered the full extent of the deceit that permeated the school system. We decided to focus on social change, diligently search to find evidence of wrongdoing, then put the pieces of the puzzle together. And we were victorious.

Our efforts allowed us to achieve major structural changes within the Los Angeles Unified School District. As part of the change, they are now required to notify all parents within seventy-two hours if any of their teachers are under investigation for suspected child abuse.

A common thread among these cases is that children and their families are afraid no one will believe them. It's a modern-day David versus Goliath scenario.

As a child, I felt that no one would believe that my father was abusing me. After all, he was a politician and major in the army. In the Miramonte case, I listened to these little girls question whether anyone would believe them. They reconnected me to the feeling of being held hostage, unable to speak—or voice my truth. They thought they would be ostracized in the community or judged negatively because they were taught to be private, to not speak about personal matters in public.

Most of us experience this type of cultural conditioning. A major impediment to bringing about necessary change is that parents are reluctant to speak publicly when institutions fail to protect their children. While many of the parents in Miramonte opted not to speak out or be filmed, a handful did. Hearing the pain in their voices and the level of trust that was lost in the educational system at large—a system my daughter is part of—was utterly devastating for me and for other parents. Restoring trust will always be a long, precarious journey, but nothing compares to living with torment for the rest of your life. By allowing them to release the anguish they have been forced to live with, justice often gives victims hope that they can create a new beginning.

At the end of the day, schools are big business, and they will fight to preserve their reputation. Ironically, around the same time that Berndt was officially accused, a sex abuse scandal at my alma mater, Penn State, rocked the university.

While not prosecuted, Joe Paterno was morally indicted in the Jerry Sandusky sex abuse scandal, while Graham Spanier, the former president of Penn State; the vice president, Gary Schultz; and the athletic director, Tim Curley, were indicted and convicted. I found myself on CNN talking as an expert about the Jerry Sandusky scandal and Joe Paterno's alleged involvement. The indictment was a major letdown. The football program was put on probation. An outside independent investigation had shown that a plethora of internal controls to detect and protect students from sex abuse were ignored by those in positions of power. This proved that sexual abuse could happen anywhere and underscored how we give those with a title a hall pass; no one pays attention to them, or people willfully ignore their actions because of their position or reputation.

Once abuse is evident, schools cover it up because they don't want the negative publicity that can affect their state and federal funding. Most of the significant decisions made by school districts are predicated upon their funding. If parents pull their children out of school, they lose money. If schools knowingly have sexual predators running around, they lose funding. Money is typically the underlying factor that fuels the code of silence. Parents worldwide fail to realize that most schools are not there to protect their children; they are there to teach them. There is a large crater between teaching and protecting, and this is the gap that I intend and work tirelessly to close.

Fear should never overpower your moral compass. If you feel something is inappropriate, it probably is. It is your duty to protect children and report it, regardless of any potential backlash. It's human nature to worry about what the future will hold, but that fear should never come before the safety of a child.

As children, we are taught by parents to obey our elders. To a certain extent, we are raised to treat strangers with dignity and respect. This level of respect is magnified when it comes to a teacher. Children are taught to revere teachers, so they aren't always aware that they are being humiliated, taken advantage of, or abused. Teachers are the epitome of authority and one of the few groups of people, outside of our parents, to whom we are taught to show the ultimate level of respect.

There is a legal doctrine when suing a school called *in loco parentis*. In Latin, this means "in (the) place of a parent." It says that schools need to be held to the same level of responsibility as a parent to their own child. We take on these cases because rarely are school administrators held to this standard.

School administrators are not in the classrooms, yet they formulate the policies, procedures, and protocols intended to safeguard kids. Because they are distanced from what's actually going on, administrators are shielded from responsibility. Because of this, when abuse cases arise, attorneys have to dig to determine who the responsible parties are. One could argue that teachers replace parents for the entirety of the school day—which equates to a significant level of influence. With that amount of power, it would be easy for anyone to misuse it, and in some instances, severely abuse it.

If a child makes a claim against an adult, do not dismiss it as harmless or attempt to justify it. Sometimes those seeking to do evil can hide in plain sight. Regardless of who it's against, any accusation should be taken seriously. If you fail to act on any accusation your child brings to you, if something significant comes of it, you are as much to blame as anyone else involved.

If you suspect that a child has been abused in any fashion, ask to fill out the form for a

SCAR. Schools typically will not volunteer the form, because they don't want SCARs. However, a parent, teacher, or doctor can fill it out and trigger an investigation. You can also file a police report if you suspect any type of child abuse. It creates a record and prompts an investigation.

Unfortunately, students in schools with large populations of children of color often experience the least protection. Miramonte, one of the largest schools in California, in 2012 had a population that was 98 percent Latino, including a significant proportion of immigrants. Sadly, students in these schools are often more easily taken advantage of. In communities that have an elevated immigrant population, parents usually have high regard for authority, particularly teachers and principals. They see them as mentors and people they admire.

When you have a school system that is heavily overpopulated and predominantly working class, mostly people of color, with a vast majority of parents working two jobs, it's no surprise that a scandal could ensue. Unfortunately for the students of Miramonte, it was the perfect storm. The size of the school alone fostered an environment where students and teachers could disappear without raising any suspicion.

Many of the children who were abused at Miramonte had working parents, so they stayed after school. If a teacher who isn't grading papers or involved in sports is hanging

around, it's important to ask why they are there after hours.

As a parent, if your child seems to have an unusual affinity toward their teacher or any other adult, don't dismiss it. Ask questions to understand why this relationship is forming and what makes it special. Understanding your child's perspective and viewing things through their lens will help you stay ahead of any situation that could develop into something inappropriate. If a child brings home a gift or mentions receiving other special attention from an adult, be concerned.

Parents should operate on the premise that they need to peek, pry, and probe. Children aren't always going to come home and tell their parents that something felt wrong, as they fear being blamed. You can't rely on children to willingly divulge information to you, and children will often be reluctant to offer up incriminating information or to divulge the "secret" an adult may have told them is just between the adult and the child.

Parent-teacher conferences and meetings with school advisors are paramount for keeping a grasp on your child. If you're not capable of attending those meetings at the scheduled

times, make a valiant effort to have someone go on your behalf or to reschedule when possible.

The question is: If we don't hold those who are responsible for molding our children to the utmost standard of professionalism and safety, who will?

For me, personally, Miramonte provided proof of what Pastor Jim and I had discussed: that if you put your Christian beliefs ahead of everything else, the fruits will come. This was the validation of that belief, and it motivated me to move forward.

16

When the system fails a child, it's difficult to understand what transpired. But witnessing a parent intentionally harm their child is unfathomable.

I wasn't raised with the normal love children deserve, and that's one of the reasons I decided to represent these types of clients and cases. On some level, I'm accustomed to witnessing evil, yet that doesn't make it any easier to process. It does, however, affirm the choice I've made.

Though every victim and every family I've represented stays with me, I have never forgotten the details from one particular case—that of Noah Cuatro. Noah's story remains embedded in my memory and continues to drive me to evoke change.

I have made it my mission to advocate for the rights of those that don't have a voice or aren't appropriately protected by the laws in our country. These laws and safety nets were created to protect children and extend beyond the roles and reach of parents. Sometimes parents are the cause of the hurt and pain children experience. That's why a system has been set in place for children when their well-being is in jeopardy.

Unfortunately, when this system is flawed, it fails the very children it was meant to safeguard against the unavoidable atrocities this world has to offer.

Four-year-old Noah Cuatro was rushed to the hospital by ambulance after his parents called 911, claiming that he had drowned. The next day, Noah was pronounced dead.

Both the hospital staff and the Los Angeles County sheriff, Alex Villanueva, stated that the claims made by Noah's parents were not consistent with the child's injuries or cause of death.

The initial report stated that Noah's death was caused by drowning in a community pool. Investigators discovered additional trauma to his body inconsistent with those claims. A physician who examined Noah said there was no indication that he drowned. They also found no water in his lungs, and his hair was not wet. The autopsy revealed that Noah died of asphyxiation and blunt-force trauma to his head. The coroner also found healing rib fractures and sexual assault trauma consistent with sodomization, among other severe injuries, on his body.

It was evident that Jose Cuatro Jr. and Ursula Juarez had brutally killed Noah. It was my team's job to prove it, and to hold them, along with the system that had repeatedly failed Noah, accountable.

Children should feel safe with their parents, but Noah was deprived of that most basic right. In many cases, children are the most vulnerable and overlooked members of our society. They may not recognize when they are being hurt or taken advantage of, and if they do, they are often too afraid to report it. The two people who should have protected Noah ultimately cost him his life.

Once a child is removed from a foster home or their parents' care, a plan of action should be set in place to ensure their safety moving forward. Noah was removed from his parents' custody multiple times but, after each occurrence, was ultimately given back to them.

The first time Noah was removed from his parents' custody was for allegations and suspicion of abuse by his mother, Ursula Juarez. She was under investigation and arrested for fracturing the skull of an infant to whom she was related. Noah had been born recently and was placed under the care of his great-grandmother Eva Hernandez.

While the court deemed Ursula unfit—claims that were substantiated by the Department of Children and Family Services (DCFS)—Noah was still released back into her custody nine months later.

When Noah was two years old, he was remanded to foster care. Michelle Thompson, cofounder of Bithiah's House, recalled how lethargic Noah was when he arrived. He was barely capable of walking. When he left their care, he was in much better spirits. They had a going-away party for Noah before he was transferred to another foster home. But ultimately, he was returned to the care of his biological parents.

Between 2018 and 2019, more than a dozen accounts of abuse and neglect were made to DCFS using the child abuse hotline. The callers believed that Noah and his siblings were all being abused. At one point, a pediatrician filed a report with child protective services stating that Noah suffered severe malnutrition. Noah was placed back into his great-grandmother's care, then, once again, returned to his parents shortly thereafter.

In February of 2019, a DCFS caseworker noted that Noah seemed lethargic and withdrawn during their interaction. Then, during March and April, there were three more accounts of abuse, including one that involved Noah showing up to Olive View–UCLA Medical Center with significant bruises on his back. On May 13, 2019, there was a report that Noah's father, Jose Cuatro, kicked Ursula and all his children while in public. The authorities were informed that Jose had an alcohol problem and was intoxicated, shouting claims that Noah was not his biological son.

Although never substantiated, the fact that Jose believed Noah wasn't his biological son could have played a significant role in the way he was treated. Our investigation revealed that Noah had sickle cell anemia, a disease commonly associated with African Americans. We believe this caused Jose to disown his son, and that Jose's resentment, coupled with Ursula's guilt, was the root of this tragedy.

After multiple reports, finally, Susan Johnson, a caseworker for DCFS, filed a twenty-six-page petition to remove Noah from his parents' custody. The petition was granted by the court, but willfully ignored by DCFS. Around this time, a family member also contacted the agency and alleged that Noah had been sodomized and had injuries to his rectum. DCFS was well aware of all the trauma Noah had been subjected to, yet they did nothing to ensure his safety or to stop the abuse and neglect from continuing.

If an allegation is made against someone in your family with respect to child safety, take it seriously. Do not disregard a claim because of your relationship with someone. We are all responsible, as adults, to ensure a child's safety if we know that it's compromised. Do your part.

After Noah's death, heavily redacted DCFS records came to light and revealed that numerous high-risk assessments of Noah's situation had been made throughout the years. Each time, it was recommended that Noah's case be promoted and action be taken. One of Noah's caseworkers stated that they had concerns about his mother's mental health, and yet nothing was done. DCFS demonstrated egregious and gross negligence, and on multiple levels were culpable for Noah's death.

Another caseworker had filed a petition to remove Noah from his parents' custody due to unsafe and dangerous conditions. Shortly after, a court order called for Noah's removal from his parents, but that was not carried out. At that time, the caseworker did not review the court order, failing Noah in the worst way.

DCFS argued that they had the discretion to not comply with the execution of Commissioner Ipson's court order. This argument was nonsensical and contradicted the whole point of DCFS getting a removal order. The social worker did the right thing, outlining the abuse and getting an emergency removal order, but the agency's higher-ups refused to execute the order—an action that would have saved Noah's life. The agency that was directly charged with protecting Noah flat-out *refused* to protect him. Instead, they offered a pathetic excuse—that the initial investigation done by Susan Johnson wasn't effective because she didn't speak Spanish. Ursula and Jose were fluent English speakers, so this should have had no bearing.

The removal order also required a forensic sexual abuse examination of Noah be conducted within seventy-two hours of the date of the order. This meant that DCFS was supposed to find Noah and take him to a forensic sexual abuse doctor. They never did that. DCFS claimed that for nearly three weeks, they couldn't find Jose and Ursula. Had they persisted, Noah would be alive today. The forensic specialist would have detected the alleged sexual abuse and Noah never would have been sent back to those two monsters. While DCFS failed to have Noah subjected to the forensic exam, they managed to make contact two weeks later. Yet all DCFS officials did was question if Noah was doing okay, then *they let him go.* They'd had two chances to save Noah Cuatro; instead, he died a month later.

In reality, DCFS didn't fulfill the removal order because they didn't want to appear as though they had done something wrong. Honoring that order would have been an admission of guilt on their part. After all, they'd had multiple chances to save Noah, but time and again had allowed him to slip out of their grasp.

While this case focused primarily on Noah, he had three other siblings who were abused and neglected as well. Unfortunately, it's not common procedure to remove all children from a household if claims are made concerning only one child, and this absolutely needs to change. If one child is being mistreated, it's almost always the case that all are, and some worse than others. Typically, evil does not discriminate—and even if it did, that should not be the assumption when it comes to the well-being of children.

With Noah, the full extent of his abuse was not revealed until after his death. He was abused and tortured at the hands of his parents for years without appropriate action being taken. DCFS had multiple opportunities to permanently remove Noah and his siblings from the house, but they chose to attend to optics, instead. They chose politics. Organizations such as DCFS are charged with defending innocent children, who typically have no one else to protect them. When mistakes or flaws in policy are discovered, they should be addressed head-on instead of covered up. Unfortunately, avoidance is commonplace in such agencies.

If you work for or with an organization that helps abused and neglected children, remember

what your oath was to them. If you suspect a child is being mistreated and it continues without any action on the matter, it is your responsibility to escalate your concerns. Whether it involves going above your superior or to other authorities, do your part.

There were documented accounts of Noah being starved for days at a time—accounts that were validated by a pediatrician, who confirmed that Noah was severely malnourished. Each of these claims was passed along to someone who could have made a lifesaving decision for Noah. Additionally, Noah had a family member disclose to DCFS that he had been penetrated anally and had pain in his rectum. Still, nothing was done on his behalf. It's unfathomable that anyone could rationalize these decisions, especially with allegations so severely disturbing in nature.

If you notice that your child has a bruise that did not happen in your care, address it immediately. Ask your child when it happened and where it came from. But be delicate with your approach, because you want them to feel comfortable telling you the truth.

If a child looks malnourished or unkempt and you have a personal relationship with them or a level of rapport that would warrant you asking

uncomfortable questions, speak to them about it. If you cannot, or if the child confirms that something is wrong at home, report the child's condition to the authorities so that they can further investigate.

DCFS's negligence cost this helpless little boy his life. Noah was described as a beautiful, joyful child with wild brown hair and a magnetic smile that could light up a room. This wonderful child's life was stolen from him; the tragedy was entirely preventable. Everything that happened to Noah, from the first documented instance of abuse all the way to his death, was avoidable. If the first claim had been handled with the level of care and urgency it deserved, Noah might be with us today.

Breaking the code of silence will not only protect children like Noah from becoming statistics and victims, it will help fix the institutions responsible for intervening and overseeing how these crimes and atrocities against children are handled.

If we can encourage and teach children to speak up about abuse, they can begin to work through the trauma sooner rather than later, avoiding greater damage. But we must remember that these are children. Their voices aren't as loud, powerful, and impactful as adults'; therefore, it is ultimately up to us.

The unfortunate reality with cases like Noah's is that it is difficult to find someone willing to speak up against their own family. In most of these situations, family members don't realize they have a case or grounds to pursue legal action. When they are finally located and approached, most don't want to get involved, even when they know a family member was liable for what transpired.

When the person you would usually notify—the parent— is the culprit, it doesn't make for an easy case to try. Regarding Noah, his siblings were the claimants for his case, as it was nearly impossible to track down his great-grandmother Eva.

I don't enjoy trying these types of cases. The reason I take them on is to shed light on the hypocrisy and mistaken ideas within a broken system. The only way to ensure this doesn't continue to happen is to educate the public. We have to rally and keep the system from disallowing the testimonies of family members. It's genuinely a criminal act. And it is equally detrimental for the other children living in an abusive household to remain there. These children are often the best or only witnesses in a case like Noah's.

DCFS followed an unfortunately common practice among such organizations, which was to announce that they were coming to interview the parents. Giving the parents time to prepare makes it impossible to ascertain what's really going on in a household or get an accurate representation of what life is like for such children.

Additionally, the system has a ridiculous policy of prioritizing reunifying families after they are separated, as opposed to looking at the evidence and making a decision that's in the best interests of the child. I have seen this happen in multiple cases, and the outcomes have been terrible for the children involved. It seems their method is to apply small Band-Aids over deep wounds. This ideology cost Noah his life, and for that reason, I will continue to seek change. As of the writing of this book, Noah's case is ongoing, and we are still in the process of fighting for him.

17

In my line of work, there are few things more sobering than coming across another case with a similar or nearly identical outcome. Noah Cuatro's case had come just on the heels of another where the agency charged with protecting a child failed miserably. That child was Anthony Avalos.

It's nearly impossible to immediately fix an entire system that's been broken for years, but you still have that small inkling of hope in the back of your mind that *this one* will be the difference maker. Although I'm confident that the work we do doesn't go unnoticed and unappreciated, it's angering to witness continual major missteps from a system designed to protect those who are incapable of protecting themselves.

Since the first child abuse case I worked on, one of the issues regarding children that I've always found concerning is when a child attempts to speak up about their troubles and their voice is silenced. Regardless of their claims, even when a child is screaming in pain or covered in scars, excuses cover up problems, hide issues, and delay saving the child. What kind of society do we live in that doesn't have time or take enough care to consistently protect our children, especially those charged to do so? And when professionals fail to do their jobs, what about the rest of us? Those who see or suspect abuse and do nothing? On a personal, humanitarian level, we owe it to children to take action.

I've accepted case after case, and they've all had similar red flags that were previously ignored—ones that could have potentially stopped the abuse in its tracks or saved lives. Because there isn't enough consistency in following the protocols set in place nor urgency to follow through on criminal charges, the child is the one that ends up paying the ultimate price of a life of trauma—struggling to overcome what was done to them— or, in the worst-case scenario, death.

Gabriel Fernandez was an eight-year-old boy who lived in Lancaster, California. As chronicled in the Netflix documentary *The Trials of Gabriel Fernandez*, Gabriel was brutally beaten, tortured, and murdered by his parents. The end of the documentary provides a glimpse into the abuse experienced by another child—ten-year-old Anthony Avalos, who lived just fifteen minutes away from Gabriel Fernandez. Eerily, Anthony had the same DCFS contact as Gabriel, and their cases had a few identical characteristics that should have caused considerable concern, immediate intervention, and action against his parents. But beyond visits and documentation, DCFS did nothing.

Anthony's was one of the most egregious cases of neglect that I have handled. During a course of sporadic supervision, including thirteen referrals for visits by DCFS to the home of Heather Barron and her boyfriend, Kareem Leiva, for more than four years the agency continually ignored or dismissed claims of abuse. Teachers, counselors, police, and relatives made at least thirteen calls to the child abuse hotline about this little boy, who never had a chance to live a happy, healthy, and normal life because he was beaten and tortured to death by his mother and her boyfriend.

The code of silence is often used by adults to protect themselves, their coworkers, their jobs, or the system, or to minimize their workload. When your job is to find the problem and you uncover evidence that something is wrong, you have to do something about it. These systems were created to save children. How can child abuse persist when several lines of defense are in place to protect them?

Despite numerous DCFS visits to the home, Anthony endured severe physical, emotional, and mental abuse. He was whipped with a belt and a looped cord, repeatedly held by his feet and dropped on his head, slammed into furniture, and locked in a room where he was unable to use the restroom for hours. He was malnourished because his food was withheld, and he endured sexual abuse. We now know that this treatment occurred for more than four years, but there is likely more that will forever remain unknown.

Over the last few days of his life, Anthony was tortured repeatedly. In addition to the repeated beatings, his eyes, nose, and mouth were sprayed with hot sauce, and Anthony was forced to kneel on dry rice for hours. His frail body was left on the floor as he shifted in and out of consciousness for more than forty-eight hours. Unable to walk or eat, this little boy went without any medical attention. On June 20, 2018, one last 911 call was made that dispatched the county sheriff. Then, on June 21, 2018, Anthony Avalos was pronounced dead at the hospital—allegedly murdered by his mother and her boyfriend.

The autopsy revealed apparent signs of sustained abuse, including significant head injuries, cigarette burns, and bruises all over his body. Similar to Gabriel Fernandez, Anthony died shortly after being admitted to the hospital. The ultimate cause of death was determined to be internal bleeding in the skull, a result of Anthony's being dropped on his head multiple times.

With at least eight documented visits and seven children in that home, one would expect DCFS to have been on high

BREAK THE CODE OF SILENCE 137

alert, keeping a close eye on the household. Yet in an appalling discovery, my team came across an audiotape that included a DCFS worker laughing about the case, stating that she had to call it in, not out of concern for the children but because it was a CYA (cover your ass) situation.

DCFS failed to ensure that Anthony was in a safe home environment with a healthy and protective parent. The majority of the notes in Anthony's file deemed that the reports of "general neglect," "severe neglect," "physical abuse," "emotional abuse," and "sexual abuse" were "unfounded" or "inconclusive," though they had all been substantiated. There was more than enough evidence to prompt the removal of every one of those children from that home and the care of their mother. Those who were responsible for protecting Anthony and who failed to do so are responsible for his death.

Los Angeles County uses Hathaway-Sycamores, a mental health and welfare agency, as an outside resource for cases like Anthony Avalos's. An intern who provided substandard counseling to Anthony and his mother was the same person who counseled Gabriel Fernandez. Interns should not be entrusted to counsel or make decisions in cases of this magnitude. The first time they worked with Anthony and his mother, the intern in question failed to disclose some of the abuse Anthony had suffered. This person was hired by the county a second time and again tasked with counseling Anthony and his mother.

Using someone who is incapable of doing a designated job perpetuates abuse. Downplaying or not taking seriously evidence of abuse lengthens the timeline over which physical and sexual abuse occurs. One more day, hour, or minute can cause a lifetime of pain or the death of yet another child. Whether a mistake stems from a lack of care or understanding, if there is a situation where undocumented abuse leads to the death of a child, the policies and guidelines that contributed to the failure must be revised. Whether the person willfully suppressed information or was incompetent, the individual responsible should be relieved of their position, or at the very least retrained. Unfortunately, within institutions such as these, one death is not enough. Instead of reassessing absolutely every policy and procedure and every person involved to ensure that avoidable mistakes like that never happen again, typically they continue with business as usual.

For a trained child care professional, there are certain situations where a definitive line should be drawn no matter what the circumstance. If someone in this position witnesses verbal or physical abuse, it is their job to report it and document the allegations and outcome appropriately. If nothing is done, they must escalate the findings until someone acts and protects the child or children. The social workers involved in Anthony's case saw his bruises and actually witnessed severe verbal abuse and threats of physical abuse while administering in-home visits. They documented those instances but did nothing to act on behalf of the children under the care of Barron and Leiva. While the focus was on Anthony's death, there were six other children in that household who were subjected to similar inhumane treatment because of inaction by social workers at DCFS.

It was also documented that Anthony had been sexually abused, and that Anthony acted out by touching one of his sisters inappropriately. Anthony and his sister shared a bedroom together and it was ordered that they should be separated, but DCFS never followed up to ensure that was done. Similar to how my father forced me to fight with my brother, Anthony was also forced to fight with his six siblings, as was Noah Cuatro.

Hate and division are taught when siblings are encouraged to harm one another. This must stop and be regarded as child abuse and child endangerment. If you see children fighting, especially in the presence of adults, report it to the authorities.

In 2014, four years before Anthony's death, Barron had been deemed by social workers to be incapable or unwilling to take care of her children and protect them from serious harm, including physical and sexual abuse. At every assessment, it was deemed that the children in Barron and Leiva's care were at high-level risk of abuse or neglect, but no one took substantial steps to prevent the abuse from continuing. And this was in the wake of the firestorm caused by the Gabriel Fernandez case. Given all the mistakes made by DCFS and others that led to Gabriel's death, why was nothing done differently to prevent an almost identical situation from causing the death of Anthony Avalos?

If you are a social worker or work in law enforcement and disclosures of abuse are made directly to you and you don't act, that could be the difference between life and death for a child. If that child had the courage to speak up about their well-being, you should fulfill your oath, code of ethics, and moral obligation to

guarantee their removal from that harmful or life-threatening environment. Had the DCFS referrals been warnings to the social worker, Anthony might have had a fighting chance at survival.

If you are a counselor or work within child protective services in any capacity and document physical or sexual abuse in a household, your objective should be to remove those children for their safety immediately. Assessments and reports should not only serve as documentation that you fulfilled a specific aspect of your job, they should be utilized to formulate and execute a plan of action for those children in need. With all the documentation and calls made to DCFS, and after social workers witnessed and completely ignored explicit verbal abuse, they failed Anthony by allowing him to remain in the home.

A parent is typically the first and primary layer of protection for any child. When they are deemed incapable or unwilling to protect their child, there shouldn't be a need for any further assessment. If you are a social worker, your job is to determine whether an environment is healthy and safe enough for a child to remain in. Once a parent cannot fulfill that duty, the next step should be placing that child

in a safer environment. While the child care system seems to be motivated to keep families together, that's not always in the child's best interest. If all signs lead to the parents not being healthy for the child, you must act swiftly to ensure their safety. Nothing else matters.

One apparent factor in Anthony's abuse that DCFS failed to significantly address was his perceived sexuality. Some of Anthony's relatives stated that his parents seemed to have intense homophobia toward him and would use explicit and derogatory language in front of other family members. Anthony's mother used the word "faggot" openly, and her boyfriend, Leiva, admitted that he didn't feel comfortable being around homosexuals. No one addressed the danger Anthony was in because of the disdain Leiva and Barron had for Anthony's perceived sexual orientation.

If someone in the home is homophobic, that is a red flag that emotional, mental, or physical abuse could be occurring.

One of Anthony's aunts, Crystal Diuguid, went on the record stating, "Part of the problem is that any time that they would come to my sister's house, they would give her a heads-up. She was able to clean her house, get groceries in her cupboard, and all of that. So I think that's [sic] one thing that needs to change is the pressure. Don't give any notice to show up." Warning someone that you're coming to do a wellness check isn't going to ensure the most authentic interaction or experience. How can you determine if they are negligent as a parent?

One of the most blatant red flags is a parent or guardian refusing a social worker access to speak with the children. It's common for children to be interviewed by a social worker separately from the parents to get an honest read on the home-life. Anthony Avalos's mother wouldn't allow the children to be interviewed without being present, and on a few occasions, completely denied social workers access to them. That should have been cause for a deeper assessment of her household or a mandate for them to be interviewed, to search for whatever she was attempting to hide. The truth is often hidden in plain sight—we have to do our part to protect the innocent. Still, even though Anthony's mother was able to cover up some of what was really going on in the house, DCFS repeatedly reported and documented that the household was unsafe.

If a family member is being abused and you do your part by reporting it, don't stop there. While you are not the legal guardian, so there is only so much you can do, you can continue to follow up. Lack of follow-through is typically how things are allowed to fall through the cracks. After they file a report or there is other documentation, many family members let the matter go, but we must do more than that. If you called child protective services, the police, or another

institution that protects children to make a complaint, continue down that road until you ensure the child's safety. We can't continue to pass on the responsibility or assume the situation is being handled appropriately.

We settled the case against the County of Los Angeles for $32 million four days before trial was set to start. We also settled with Hathaway-Sycamores for an undisclosed amount of money.

There is a code of silence in the DCFS, in school districts, private and public universities, county agencies, police departments, churches, government agencies, and other organizations, and we need to apply concerted effort to break that code of silence. We must do a better job of protecting our children, and ensure that when something happens, they feel safe to speak up.

18

Since I transitioned to predominantly representing victims of child abuse, my lens has refocused considerably. I no longer operate solely from an attorney's perspective, but also as a vigilant, caring father. Clients don't come to me because I'm competitive, but because I can relate to them on multiple levels. Not only did I live some of the trauma I work to alleviate, but also I have a daughter that I'm driven to protect with my life. Every child and every situation I encounter reminds me of the unrelenting work necessary to keep my daughter safe. With every case, I ask myself two questions: Would you want this to happen to your child? What can you do to stop this from happening again?

As I've learned, some of these cases are bigger than the victims. This is not meant to diminish the horror they've endured, but to put into perspective the responsibility and duty we have as a team. We have the power, opportunity, and platform not just to receive justice for one victim, or even one group of victims, but to create change to keep history from repeating itself. The Santa Monica Police Activities League case was one such instance.

Eric Uller terrorized hundreds of young children in Santa Monica, California, from 1989 to the early 2000s. He was employed by the City of Santa Monica as its IT director, and he regularly volunteered in the Police Activities League (PAL)—an after-school program—that gave him direct access to teenage boys.

In 2018, a forty-two-year-old man who had been molested by Uller as a teen while attending the PAL program approached me and asked me to represent him. The victim was courageous enough to participate in a press conference in front of Santa Monica City Hall, which opened the floodgates. After they saw this brave man make his public statement, a deluge of other victims came forward. I have now represented over fifty of Eric Uller's victims.

As with the Miramonte case, we still had to prove that the police department "knew" or "should have known" that Eric Uller was molesting children. In 2019, after my initial client came forward, the LA County Sheriff's Department launched an investigation. They discovered that Uller had walked a kid attending PAL to a shed where they stored lawnmowers and allegedly fondled him—a complaint that had been registered with the city and the PAL program back in the 1990s. That proved they were on notice that Uller was a risk but they deliberately ignored that fact, further enabling his behavior.

Uller had an unassuming, meek demeanor. He gained trust with the PAL kids through a grooming process in which he bought clothing, food, pagers, skateboards, and video games for the children, took them to LA Dodgers games, and gave them money. Uller would give his victims twenty or forty dollars, then tell them that they would get in trouble if they told anyone. In some instances, he told the kids that their parents would get deported.

Uller wore a badge, carried a gun, and had a police transmitter inside his black-and-blue Suburban. Understandably, his victims thought he was a police officer—and for all intents and purposes, he played the role perfectly. He used his unmarked police-issue vehicle to extend rides home to his teenage victims. First, he'd allege that they needed a medical exam or physical to continue involvement with PAL. Then, promising that nurses would be there, Uller used his father's medical office or his car to sexually assault these young boys. Uller's former boss reported seeing him with young teenage boys all over town, yet he opted to ignore this red flag. In spite of documented complaints and obviously questionable behavior, there was no formal investigation by Santa Monica until child pornography found on a police department computer screen was linked back to Uller.

Delayed action after an accusation is a common occurrence in cases like this. Records come to light and witnesses begin recanting their statements, coming up with different versions of the truth. It becomes apparent that there were multiple opportunities for people who witnessed questionable behavior to officially report and investigate it. But in organizations whose members have pledged allegiance to one another, such as police organizations, the code of silence is more important than protecting the children in their care. By being willfully ignorant and not following protocol, they protect and serve their own at the cost of innocent victims.

Whenever there is a report of sexual abuse, I believe it should be mandated that an independent person or agency conduct the investigation. Far too often, a victim's claim does not hold enough weight to warrant immediate corrective action internally. The built-in conflict of interest means you can't trust the people who allow these atrocities to happen to investigate them appropriately. The sheriff's report for the Santa Monica case showed that they knew what was going on but didn't say anything about it. After that first documented complaint, Uller was allowed to molest young boys for nearly

another twenty years before being arrested. Why would anyone want to protect a man like that? More importantly, why
would anyone ignore an accusation of that magnitude?

**It is our civic duty to be both prudent and
persistent when bringing forth such serious
allegations. If there isn't immediate action from
the person you report to, go above them. When
adults are sexually inappropriate with children,
especially in large systems like an after-school
program, you can expect pushback. What you
can't do is stop at the first roadblock. If you do,
you are leaving a child's life in the hands of a
system designed to protect its own and minimize risk.**

As I mentioned previously, many of the cases I handle in-
volve victims from underprivileged communities, and this was
one such case. Most of the children Uller assaulted lived in the
less affluent, predominantly Latino, Pico area of LA County.
Targeting these children is a tactic that allows a predator to
lure their prey without much resistance or awareness that
grooming is taking place. Children often can't fully compre-
hend when they are being taken advantage of or violated. In
many cases, even when they do understand, they fear the consequences of speaking their truth. Imagine being a thirteen-
year-old boy from a modest- to low-income household, perhaps
with immigrant parents, faced with the prospect of reporting
a police officer for fondling you. Who would believe you?

It is hard for children to come forward, as they have been groomed to think they are reporting a nice person. Further, when the abuser is of the same sex, these children sometimes begin to question their sexuality, and they don't want to address that. Their embarrassment is tremendous. Many of the male victims we represented disclosed to their therapists that they enjoyed the feeling evoked during the molestation. This created confusion in the minds of these kids, which is exactly what a sexual predator wants. The confusion created a barrier to the disclosure of the abuse.

This lawsuit offered victims a platform. The case's high visibility helped give those whose story would have otherwise remained untold the courage to come forward with confidence that justice would be served. I represented nineteen of the initial twenty-four victims in the Santa Monica PAL case. Not one of them had ever disclosed the abuse to anyone, not even to their spouse. When boys are molested, regardless of their cultural background, it is the ultimate defamation of their character and manhood. In general, we raise young boys to be ultratough and devoid of emotion. I would have been afraid to tell my dad if a grown man had molested me. Though not always intentional, we instill this attitude and behavior in boys, and it must change. The clients I've represented felt that no one would believe them, treat them the same way, or want to talk about it had they reported it immediately, and I've seen that across multiple other cases as well.

We must do a better job helping boys shed their tough exterior and encouraging them to be honest about what they are feeling and experiencing. If they feel it could strip them of their

manhood, they are less likely to speak up if something happens.

Pay attention to your child's demeanor or any changes to their typical routine. When it comes to identifying underlying issues, the task can be complicated, as children will usually attempt to hide them. If someone is sexually assaulting your child, there will be signs displayed that indicate the need for more in-depth conversations. Ask specific questions or take them to a professional for an assessment; they may feel more comfortable talking to a therapist or counselor. It is detrimental to your child's well-being to overlook behavioral changes to avoid having an uncomfortable discussion. As parents, it's our responsibility to protect our children—with our lives if necessary.

One of the most common changes in behavior is the child being withdrawn, not talking as much as they usually would. Night terrors, decreased confidence, a change in eating habits, excessive worry, and increased aggression are some other issues that should alert you that something may be going on. Again, most children won't go to their parents when something as devastating as sexual assault occurs, because of their embarrassment. They are

often confused or feel that they did something
to deserve what is happening to them or have
been told that they must keep it a secret or
something bad will happen, which is why it can
go on for years.

Ultimately, your child's safety is strength-
ened by the conversations you have with them
at an early age. It's imperative to be transparent with your children about how the world
works. Keeping them in the dark will only be
detrimental to their overall growth. While not
everyone is out to get them, they need to understand that they won't always be treated with
the love and respect they deserve. As a parent,
you must advocate for your children and raise
them to trust you. Engage in those awkward
conversations about what is inappropriate and
how other adults should treat them. These honest conversations about the harsh reality they
live in can be the difference maker, giving them
the discernment necessary to navigate the evil
that lurks among us.

To add insult to injury, when victims come forward, society sometimes accuses them of doing it for money. From being
in the trenches for the last twelve years, I have seen over and
over that, sadly, money matters far more to many institutions

than doing the right thing. Therefore, the only way to get real, systemic change is to hit them where it hurts—in the pocketbook. Getting multimillion-dollar settlements and verdicts against government entities and private organizations is not about greed, but about making them answer to the taxpayers. It is about accountability. Litigation is the search for the truth. It creates awareness and transparency and brings about social change. When I do press conferences, publicly exposing abuse that has been covered up, it forces the institutions involved to answer to the public.

I can't do anything about the years I lived in fear as a child, but I'm not afraid to go after institutions, abusers, and predators now. This work, though rewarding, is draining, lonely, and daunting—but this is what other victims feel when they try to come out with their truth. By the time they reach me, they feel defeated, so it's up to my team and me to help them change their mindset. I have to disarm their helplessness, fear, and belief that no one will protect them. We go on a journey with our clients. We serve as their therapists, counselors, and mentors as they endure the painful ordeal of recounting their experiences.

When I was on the phone with a victim from the PAL case, he gave me an in-depth, accurate depiction of what happened to him. I spent forty-five minutes listening, caring, and validating. As a client's legal representation, it's essential that I not only grasp the severity of the details they are recounting, but truly hear them. They are often afraid people will think they are weird or strange. Given what I went through as a child, I can understand that. Though it's difficult to listen to their pain, I see what they are trying to cope with in their attempt to live a normal life, and I feel confident in leading them in the appropriate direction to get help.

I've had victims who can't hold down a job. Who have trouble maintaining normal, healthy relationships or allowing anyone to get close. I had a client who didn't trust a single person, not even a therapist. This is the harsh reality for children who grow up dealing with trauma. I can't take their pain away, but I can try to get them the justice they deserve.

When it came to the legal case, PAL operated with corrupt intentions, failing to come clean. The money they received from the city and state was tied to the number of children in the program, so they opted to do unconstitutional things to keep the public from hearing the reality of the tragic situation. This included attempting to gag lawyers so we couldn't publicly discuss the case, which is unethical. They also didn't want to acknowledge any victims outside the initial twelve, and they tried to keep us from finding additional claims. But we did anyway, uncovering a broader pattern of abuse than we first realized.

Once the first nine victims told their stories, a tenth surfaced, but with a different abuser. Elizabeth Esquivias claimed that for two years, from ages twelve to thirteen, she had been repeatedly sexually assaulted by another PAL worker, Fernando Ortega. Ortega's job was to drive the children home after the program. Esquivias claimed that he would intentionally drop her off last, which allowed them to be alone, resulting in at least five incidents of assault.

The first few victims caused a domino effect, inciting nearly a dozen others to bring forth their allegations. This often occurs with a case involving multiple victims. Elizabeth had a brother whom Eric Uller assaulted. Had she not felt that she had a safe outlet to tell her story, her brother might have continued to hold on to his secret, the same way she did for so many years. Her strength compelled her brother to talk about the atrocities he experienced, which allowed me to file my fourth complaint.

This particular case placed the majority of focus on the primary suspect, Eric Uller, since he assaulted many more children—but Ortega's role cannot go overlooked. He had a criminal arrest record and was on probation at the time of his offenses. That poses the question: What steps were taken by the City of Santa Monica and PAL to ensure that Ortega was mentally fit to care for children? Especially in a capacity as intimate as driving them home after the program. If they did execute their due diligence and were aware of Ortega's criminal background, why, with a known arrest record, was he allowed to care for children?

Having multiple abusers terrify children under the same roof is horrible—but having an abuser with an arrest record slip through the cracks is entirely unacceptable. Elizabeth could have potentially avoided this childhood trauma if Ortega had been vetted appropriately. And if Uller had gone through an in-depth psychological evaluation, there might have been signs that indicated he had a sickness concerning children. There must be a more vigorous and intense process for setting mandatory qualifications to mentor, teach, or work with children in any official capacity. Again, children rely on us for their protection, so we must commit to being their voices and advocates.

PAL programs exist nationwide, and police departments partner with nonprofit agencies to create them. If your child is participating in a Police Activities League, it's paramount that you know who the volunteers are and do your due diligence as a parent to make your presence known. It's important to know who is supervising the volunteers. When you see someone like an Eric Uller pack five teenage boys,

ages thirteen to fifteen, in a van to get tacos, it might prove prudent to inquire if something inappropriate is going on.

Unfortunately, it's nearly impossible to completely protect your child when they aren't in your physical presence. We have to place trust in school systems, day cares, coaches, and after-school programs run by adults that we barely know. These types of programs are usually the only option for single-family households or parents who need assistance. Make sure you get to know these individuals and inquire about their backgrounds. Do random, unscheduled visits to ensure your child is treated properly and is in a safe environment. Children from households that don't have the necessary support are prime victims of these sexual predators.

One potential ally that is often overlooked is the media. Journalists can obtain public records of arrest (PRAs) without any pending litigation or criminal investigation. If there is no pending investigation of a sexual predator or civil case, and your child was subject to an assault, you can go to a reporter and ask them to make a Public Records Act request. They can retrieve records the rest of us cannot access, because it's their right. These reports can be a significantly helpful tool in catching a predator.

Predators are like drug addicts. They never molest just one child, and there will be multiple reports. Like Mark Berndt from Miramonte, the predators in the Santa Monica case had sexually assaulted their victims for twenty years. You have to assume these suspected child molesters have done it before and will do it again.

> **If you need help supporting your claim, get the media involved, file a lawsuit, and try to get a subpoena to retrieve that information. The media can take a protective stance for you and your child.**

Once the Santa Monica PD's failure to take action and the attempted cover-up were made public, it spurred outrage in Santa Monica. The case also shed light on the overwhelming disparity in the treatment of children in the community, with those who are underprivileged receiving little attention. As of the time of this book, my team has been able to recover $42 million on behalf of forty-five victims, without litigating the case. Eric Uller died by suicide before going to trial We represent an additional 35 victims in ongoing litigation.

No amount of money can erase what these victims endured, but it can help validate their experiences—show them that, finally, someone heard and believed them. And it can help force changes in the system to prevent future victimization and cover-ups.

19

The foster care system was created in the nineteenth century to solve a significant problem in the United States—finding homes for children who were abandoned, whose parents died, or who for other reasons had nowhere to go. Children needed places to take them in, keep them safe, and care for them. At that time in New York, that need was significant. Around 30,000 children were living in the streets and the slums. Due to this ongoing, worsening issue, around 1853, Charles Loring Brace conceptualized an idea to move these displaced children from the streets to families that willingly wanted to care for them. Early on, he realized there was a solution that would benefit children living on the streets and loving families that either couldn't have children of their own or lost them tragically.

Before his death, through his selfless efforts, Brace transported approximately 200,000 children to new lives. It was termed the Orphan Train movement, as he sent all the children via train to their new families. After Brace's passing, his son continued his work, and the program was further adapted and transformed into the adoption and foster care system that we know today.

According to a report by the US Department of Health and Human Services (October 2021), 30 percent of children in the foster care system are between six and twelve, and 27 percent are aged thirteen to twenty. Many of these children will have three or more placements in different homes within two years. Brace's intent from the very beginning was to do good in society. Unfortunately, somewhere along the way, the system shifted into one that does not always have children's best interests at heart.

The problem stems from the overwhelming number of children who are in the foster care system. At the time of this writing, more than 400,000 children are in the care of foster homes in the United States. Though these homes are intended to provide safe harbor, the unfortunate truth is that a significant number of children placed into foster care to escape their harsh realities are actually placed into more-dire situations. Foster care has transitioned from a well-intentioned effort into a global business—one driven by bottom lines and profitability.

As it stands, most foster care centers are incentivized to have children in their custody. Once a child is placed with a family for adoption or a permanent custodianship, or reintegrated with their biological parents, the payments for that child stop. The system actually benefits from having children remain in foster care rather than be adopted or returned to their biological families. Rewarding foster care centers for retaining children is not the answer. A simple fix would be to reverse the incentive and only remit payments once those children are placed into a healthy, permanent situation.

When it comes time to place a child in a foster home, the safety and best interest of the child should always come first. But there are several problems inherent in the system that result in kids not being put first or cared for appropriately. One of them is lowered standards for individuals to become social workers. Their job is paramount to ensuring the child's safety not only when they are being placed but throughout that child's stay. Yet the quality of social workers is being lowered so that more can be hired in an attempt to keep up with the number of children in the system.

Then there are problems with the system itself. Without the appropriate procedures in place, it's impossible to adequately protect these innocent children. Lack of execution of the policies meant to protect kids, coupled with financial incentives to keep kids in foster care, has created a vicious cycle—one that I have personally witnessed for decades. One of the worst parts of taking on child abuse cases is seeing just how many people along the way could have prevented or stopped the abuse. Instead, they didn't, and so they are responsible for what these children went through.

Several years ago, I handled a case that included eight children, some siblings, who were molested, beaten, starved, assaulted, and tortured by their foster caregivers over seven years. This case specifically was a clear indication of the procedures that fail to assure accountability for children.

Lisa Oates and Nawab Wilson were entrusted by Interim Care Foster Family Agency, a private foster agency, and San Bernardino County's Child Protective Services (CPS) to provide foster care. Over seven years, Oates and Wilson were evicted for nonpayment from four different homes. They were even homeless for a period of time. The very first eviction was a red flag, signaling to Interim that something was wrong, but it was ignored. Additionally, when Interim's social workers went out to the homes, they weren't keeping a log of what was going on or what conversations were had. That's one of the reasons Oates and Wilson were able to beat the system for seven years.

These types of agencies need to be monitored, because unlike most foster agencies, they aren't directly supervised by the government. Over and over, the people Interim hired to administer their program failed miserably, and their severe mishaps were overlooked. Repeatedly, policies were disregarded that they had set in place to ensure this type of scenario would not occur.

Like many private child care agencies, Interim was engaged in an underhanded system of "cash for kids." They do it for the money. When families get these children, they get money. In essence, the adoption turns into a money-making machine for the foster parents, as they receive a stipend when a private adoption agency is involved. This is the draw and common denominator. By fostering eight children, Oates and Wilson were making a significant amount of money.

Oates took the money and started a preschool childcare program in her home. While parents paid her to take care of their children, she starved her foster kids—all the foster children in the couple's care were severely undernourished. The foster parents would reportedly eat a steak or substantial meals in front of the children, then give them a can of soup that had been open for days. Oates and Wilson monitored what was in the pantry, and the children were whipped or beaten if they took anything. The children had to steal food from the neighboring 7-Eleven store to survive because they weren't given money for lunch, though the stipend Oates and Wilson received for their care was meant for precisely those types of expenses.

If you, as a single parent, bring a new boyfriend or girlfriend into the house, be conscious of your children's behavior. If they become disruptive or have a significant change in their demeanor, they could be acting out to ask for help. Remember, children don't always know

how to communicate what they feel or what was done to them. As a parent, if you allow someone around your child who is harming them, your child may blame you because you've given that person permission and set the tone by bringing them into your house.

Interim failed to supervise their foster parents properly. Oates and Wilson were able to operate seven uncertified facilities (foster homes) without Interim visiting the facilities or maintaining any semblance of communication or physical contact with them. Interim breached not only the trust of these children, but also their judiciary commitment and oath. They were beyond negligent.

A foster care agency may not know when a foster family has been evicted. If you see this occur, that is a massive red flag. Do not assume the agency knows—call and file a report.

Meanwhile, eight innocent children were beaten with belts, made to walk miles to the laundromat while carrying plastic bags containing clothing, and intentionally forced to wear ill-fitting clothing for humiliation, among other repugnant acts. They were made to squat while holding two cans of paint, which caused physical and mental harm. They couldn't take a break and drop to their knees. The children were also forced to walk two miles to school because Oates wouldn't allow them to take the bus, and were made to fight one another.

It's unlikely that no one outside the family ever witnessed these horrible occurrences. Nothing about these actions was normal, and it's shameful and disturbing that no adult outside Interim or CPS stepped in to help these children.

There will be times when making the right moral call will make you feel as though you're on an island—in some cases, you might be. But knowing that you did everything in your power against the majority will always feel right in the end, as it will protect children, potentially even saving their lives.

Despite multiple opportunities to address their missteps, Interim continued to certify individuals who had absolutely no business supervising children, and they continued to collect a paycheck.

In the end, we were able to secure a $6.5 million settlement against Interim Care Foster Family Agency.

If you work for an organization involved in ensuring the safety and well-being of children, your responsibility extends beyond your job. If you witness violations in other areas of the operation but ignore them, you are part of the

problem. We all have to do our part to ensure the children we are sworn to protect actually stay protected under our care.

In another case involving the foster care system, one of my plaintiffs, Deandre Jones, reported serious allegations to the counselor assigned to his foster home. He told Dr. Maurizio Assandri that two of the other children in the house were suffering from severe neglect, hunger, and sleep deprivation, and were made to engage in nightly labor. The kids were required to stay up until nearly five in the morning cleaning the house, leaving them with only an hour or two of sleep. Deandre's accounts, by all standards, should have warranted an immediate investigation for suspected child abuse. The report alone should have mandated Dr. Assandri to bring forth those allegations, yet he failed to do so. Two of the kids ran away, ended up at a bus stop, and were found by adults who, fortunately, did the right thing and called the sheriff. The sheriff went to the house and removed the rest of the kids.

Treat every foster child as if they were your own, and listen to their allegations. Would you be dismissive if your child came to you with abuse allegations? Would you not follow the protocol perfectly to ensure that it was looked into immediately and rectified if need be? That is the level of concern that every child deserves.

If you don't follow up on a claim made by a

child, they will more than likely never confide in you again. Don't underestimate the courage it takes for them to come to you with a serious claim of abuse.

———————————————

Unfortunately, the mistreatment of children is a seriously understated international issue. Children continue to be taken advantage of by the adults meant to protect and shield them from harm. Do foster care centers like Interim have a foundation of genuine concern for the children they house? Or are they simply "cash for kids" operations that will continue to exploit innocent children for millions and billions of dollars? We all need to unite and stay vigilant to protect these children.

20

Civil rights attorneys like me work tirelessly to evoke change within systems that directly affect children—or anyone who can't protect themselves. We work diligently to expose any potential threats from the people and places we trust to safeguard our children and loved ones from the horrors in this world. In most cases, the majority of people in these organizations attempt to do their jobs to the best of their ability, with the utmost respect. Yet sometimes people abuse this trust and use their access or status, or the positive reputation of the department or organization, to prey on the vulnerable.

Unfortunately, there are certain people and organizations that we trust unquestioningly even when their behavior does not live up to our standards or their positive reputation. Although schools, foster homes, and even family members have sexually assaulted or done other terrible things to children, we tend to believe that it won't happen to *our* children. That isn't due to a lack of care and concern for our children, but rather a certain level of expectation for the individuals who teach and mentor them. We think that one bad apple doesn't spoil the bunch, that one or two cases of abuse are a fluke. Many of us are guilty of assuming the positive intent of the people in these positions of power, and we must shift that mentality—it's long overdue.

I've witnessed these atrocities firsthand and fought for hundreds of children, yet I still give the systems designated to serve my daughter a fair chance. We can't allow every terrible thing we see or hear about to taint our perception of everyone. There are exceptional teachers, administrators, mentors, tutors, community leaders, and others working hard to help children learn and develop. However, we must remain vigilant and flush out those who wish to harm children. We must remove them from positions of authority over children and hold them accountable in a civil court. And we must do the same with those who work to conceal all forms of abuse, violence, discrimination, hate, and bullying. We must demand that we are kept well informed of anything that could adversely affect children, so we can protect our kids.

Due to the reputation my firm has garnered over the years, there has been a significant progression in the types of cases and victims I represent. Miramonte was my first high-profile case, and from that, people began to see my firm as a respectable, trustworthy practice that can handle such complex, far-reaching cases. Most recently, I have teamed up with and begun representing multiple clients from the Boy Scouts of America (BSA) case, which at the time of this writing is still in litigation. We are co-counsel for more than two hundred Boy Scouts who were victims of sexual abuse. There are thousands of victims in this case, and every one of them is a unique individual. The case also spans multiple abusers over different periods of time.

BSA is a prime example of an organization that most would assume to be a safe place for their children. They are known for having high standards not only for their participants, but for the Scout leaders involved in the lives of these children. Prior to these abuse cases, BSA had an exemplary reputation with the public. The organization was established in 1910 and has accumulated more than 110 million participants. Their stated mission is to "prepare young people to make ethical and moral choices over their lifetimes by instilling in them the values of the Scout Oath and Law." They were considered an organization where children developed outdoor skills and values such as good citizenship and trustworthiness on their journey to adulthood.

For a few reasons, in 2019, BSA restructured their organization. First, they changed their name from Boy Scouts of America to BSA, ostensibly to align with the institutional change that allowed girls to join separate gender-specific groups within BSA. But it could have been due to earlier lawsuits, the current global lawsuit, or other organizational changes. They also filed a Chapter 11 bankruptcy to begin a reorganization of their finances to accommodate the nearly 93,000 former Scouts who filed claims of sexual abuse.

If you are a victim of sexual abuse, most often you will not be alone. While it takes courage to deal with it head-on, know that you will have support. It won't always come from those you would expect, but when you step forward to walk in your truth, there will be people like me who have vowed to avenge the transgressions against you to the best of our abilities. You won't be in the fight alone.

To witness the demise of an organization like BSA, which has been around for more than one hundred years, is surreal. As an attorney, I don't typically make all-inclusive statements, but we can assume that almost everyone, at one point, thought very highly of the BSA. It was a place where young people looked forward to learning something paramount while approaching adulthood. Furthermore, it was a place where parents believed their children would learn skills beyond what they might be able to provide. And from the outside, it appeared *safe*. But far too many within the organization have used the once-positive reputation of BSA as a shield to perpetrate abuse, and far too many others have either deliberately ignored their trespasses or engaged in cover-ups. My firm is working to ensure that the abuse that former Scouts suffered is revealed, and we are working to force institutional change so that it doesn't happen again.

An institution that plays a role in shaping and molding your children should never be trusted based solely on its history. You should be satisfied only when you've successfully done your due diligence, whether that's research or attending events firsthand, to comfortably and accurately assess their ability to protect your child.

If you work for a large organization and hear about misconduct taking place, there are whistleblower hotlines available to allow you to safely and anonymously file a complaint. If you are retaliated against for filing an internal

complaint, you have federal protection in court against your employer. It is your duty to ensure that information is delivered to someone you trust will take it seriously. Often, staff will protect their own. When working for an organization like BSA, your loyalty and "oath" should not be to the company, but to the children you were sworn to protect and care for.

If you work in a leadership capacity, it's your moral responsibility to demand immediate systemic change within your organization before and once sexual abuse occurs under your watch. Not only should you implement safeguards to ensure it doesn't happen again, but you should look at how it transpired in the first place. Do not be dismissive of abuse.

Sadly, I have often been accused of being a money chaser, because my firm seeks to secure significant monetary settlements. I have said it before, but I will repeat it because it is so important. *Money brings change.* If we didn't receive major financial awards, most of these organizations would never change, and children would continue to be victimized. It's unfortunate that it takes money to force change—that the awareness of the abuse, itself, isn't motivation enough to prompt organizations to change. But it's not. And so firms like mine will continue to hold them accountable, and to do what it takes to ensure that the broken systems that perpetuate abuse are fixed.

Many of the institutions designed to support children have one common theme—the children who come to them are already in a situation that makes them inherently more vulnerable or susceptible to becoming a target for a predator. Children who are preyed upon often come from a household consisting of a single parent. Sometimes they are already products of mental, physical, emotional, or sexual abuse. Whatever the situation may be, it makes the children more likely and easier to be targeted for abuse. This is why safeguards must be put in place within every organization to ensure that children from all ethnicities, backgrounds, and walks of life are protected, especially when the children are from particularly vulnerable populations.

As parents—especially if we are single parents—we are often excited to have a mental and physical break from the demands of raising children. The BSA is one of many organizations that helps to alleviate some of the parenting stress, if even just for the summer or weekends. Sometimes the trust we put in these organizations is warranted, but we need to be diligent in asking our children about their time away and how they were treated. Don't be afraid to ask if anything that didn't feel normal occurred while they were there. Children tend to hold on to something dramatic, especially abuse, and rarely tell you directly. You have to care. You have to ask.

If you are a single parent, know that it is okay to ask for help. You can't do it all by yourself. It's been said that it takes a village to raise a child. While not everyone has access to a village, utilize those within your network that have proven they are trustworthy to you and your children. You won't always be able to do random spot checks on your children due to the demands placed on you to be a responsible parent, but it is in your best interest to have someone designated in that role to ensure their safety.

Considering the enormity of the BSA's internal issues, it is my hope that they are attempting to figure out where this widespread problem started at the foundational level. Civil lawsuits actually help institutions like the BSA learn how to safeguard kids, because as part of the investigation, we help uncover the cracks in the internal controls, making it easier to fix them. The process brings awareness of the breakdown in the internal protocols and procedures. For an organization built on teaching young children life principles, the BSA was clearly not executing their own appropriately, especially in the selection of candidates for youth volunteers. We are helping these agencies help themselves to protect kids.

PART IV

BREAKING THE CODE OF SILENCE: WARNING SIGNS OF CHILD ABUSE

21

Each of us has a unique narrative that began with childhood. For some, it may not have any of the abuse, pain, suffering, or horror that others have experienced. Others may have situations that were unpleasant, but overall, their life has been good. Regardless of how you identify with your own story or history, don't let it remove you from having compassion and empathy for others, especially children.

It's often said that whatever we go through is not meant to destroy us, it's meant to make us stronger. That is a great thing to know when you're an adult, adequately equipped with the ability and resources to rebound and heal from trauma and pain. But for defenseless children, a maxim like this is inadequate, and we have to provide more. We think that children will outgrow their pain and simply forget. We minimize and justify the atrocities done to them. But for many, it can affect their mental, emotional, and physical health over the long term; cause anxiety, depression, PTSD; and contribute to increased substance abuse and suicide. Our youth are subjected to hormones, bullying, and pressure from social media—a perfect storm for self-doubt. When there is another layer, a layer of child abuse, that could be the tipping point for them to do something drastic. Sexual trauma can cause borderline personality disorder (BPD). The point is that children will not escape harmful behaviors and history, and they won't forget. They may bury it—but they will never forget. Why let them ever get to that point? Why would you chance this?

The cases I've handled over the years have given me uncommon insight into the mindset of victims. I have not only gained a better understanding of the reasons they've held on to these horrendous encounters but, more importantly, I've also learned how they were coerced into these situations, why they trusted the individuals who took advantage of them, and what warning signs or red flags were present but ignored. It's allowed me to develop a keen ability to relate to any victim I represent as well as my daughter and others who are potential victims. I am thankful and hopeful that every case brings us one step closer to putting a complete stop to the abusers out there and the institutions that enable this destructive behavior. And I want to put my experience and insight to further use in stopping or preventing abuse, by sharing it with you.

I often say that if you show me a case of abuse, I'll show you red flags. Throughout parts II and III of this book, I've highlighted some of those warning signs, and now I want to underscore some of them again. These are among the most common red flags that I have seen over and over again in my work, and I share them not with an intention of making you fearful, but of empowering you, and helping to make you aware so that, together, we can stop abuse, or better yet, prevent it from happening at all.

I also want to underscore that it should not just fall to parents to be vigilant. Children are our shared responsibility, whether they are ours or someone else's. We *all* need to pay attention, not just to our own lives, but to anyone and everyone who is vulnerable, especially children. We all have a stake in one another. I know that it can be uncomfortable at times to ask questions. I know that for many of us, we feel maxed out just trying to care for ourselves or our own children. But we need to expand our circle of care.

It's about *we*, not me.

Below you'll find a list of warning signs that can help alert you that something may be wrong, along with general issues to consider when it comes to ensuring children's welfare. But I can sum up the most important takeaway with one sentence:

If you see or sense that something is wrong, *do something*.

Take action. Don't question. Don't wait. Investigate. Report it. And follow up.

If parents are not doing what is required to protect the children in their care, or if they may be the abusers themselves, create a paper trail. If the teacher or administrator isn't doing what they should, create a paper trail. Regardless of who it is, create a paper trail whenever a child is being treated inappropriately or concerns about their treatment are being mishandled. It's evidence.

Children can survive abuse and go on to heal, and to live happy and productive lives, if they make it that far. But the reality is that countless children do not survive. *Anthony and Noah did not.*

Do not be dismissive when someone brings something to your attention that seems uncharacteristic of another individual. Do you really know everything about that person? *Are you sure?* Separate out what you actually know for a fact about that person, and what you merely hope is true. Take the time to investigate the situation further or engage the proper authorities to do so, and—I'll say it again—create a paper trail.

Don't encourage children not to tell their truth, especially if it is harmful to them. This is the beginning of breaking the code of silence. And after you take that first step to save a child or protect another human being, please follow up. The space between your call and inactivity can cost a child their life. *It does every day.*

COMMON RED FLAGS

First and foremost, we must resolve to use our judgment and be more involved with our children, their lives, and the decisions they are making when they aren't within our grasp. Problems arise when we, as parents, allow our children to be *parented* by teachers, family friends, mentors, and anyone else with whom a child typically forms a bond at a young age. We assume positive intent, and in some cases that can make us ignore our perceptions that something is not right.

Children are incredibly impressionable, especially at a young age. With that in mind, it's imperative that we form a significant bond built on trust during the years that matter most. Regardless of their intent, no one will love and care for our children more than we should. We must practice due diligence from the onset of our children's introduction to the real world. Consistent engagement and attention could save them from the horrors lurking in the shadows that they will inevitably encounter, regardless of our love for them. Being aware of these threats to their safety allows us to equip our children with the wisdom to navigate these challenges.

Be cautious and vigilant as a parent, nonparent, guardian, grandparent, or caring neighbor. The cautions and advice I provide below are framed for parents, but can apply to anyone who cares for or otherwise spends time around children. Take a stake in these kids even if you are not a parent—be the third set of eyes. When it comes to children, never be dismissive of behaviors that would otherwise seem inappropriate just because you think you know the individual in question. Instead, please ask qualifying and appropriate questions to ensure a child's safety. You are the child's first line of defense. It's better to be overly cautious than allow a child to become damaged for life, be murdered, or die by suicide.

Also, keep the lines of communication open. You want to provide a safe space for kids and, as much as possible, have them be comfortable talking to you.

That said, here are some of the broader red flags to look out for, and considerations to keep in mind with regard to child safety.

Unusual Behavior by Teachers or Staff

Parents, get a sense of whether anyone at your child's school (including after-school programs) or other activities may be acting inappropriately. For example, ask your child if they favor any teachers or staff, or if they're spending more time with a teacher or staff member than is required by normal activities. A teacher may keep photos of certain students on their desk or give special notes or cards to some students. Teachers should not be communicating with students through private notes. Also, if a teacher or other adult is giving your child gifts or money, offering them rides home, or otherwise showing a special interest in your child, that is a major red flag. Of course you want to be able to trust the people who are tasked with caring for, educating, or mentoring your child, but try not to let that cloud your judgment.

Most child sexual predators in teaching roles are well liked by the students. That is also part of the grooming formula. Most children and even parents think this is okay, or even good, because they instruct their children to revere teachers. We need to be far more cynical and vigilant about teachers and stop placing them in such high regard, because it puts blinders on children and parents. It makes it harder to report a nice teacher who gives out cool notes and cards and takes a personal interest in your child. Similarly, be wary of any teacher showing up to watch any of your child's extracurricular activities. Be cautious of a teacher who wants to take the parents out to lunch or grab a beer with Dad.

While we don't want to dissuade teachers from being kind to and inspiring for our children, we need to establish boundaries regarding what is professional and what becomes too personal. Being a teacher with hundreds of children around every day is the perfect "playground for predators." Parents need to start seeing it from *that* standpoint. There is no better place to go than a school to groom, manipulate, and molest children. Teachers are assumed to be leaders in the community.

Make sure your child does not undergo any type of physical performed by a school staff member or a member of an after-school program. Get your child a physical through your family pediatrician. It's very easy for abusers to touch children inappropriately at these types of physicals, and for the child to not necessarily know any better. Also, find out if teachers or other school staff are engaging in unusual activities, such as closing their window blinds or locking the door during class. This could be a signal of a teacher concealing nefarious conduct.

When your child is younger, entering preschool, kindergarten, and even first grade, you should study the interior of their classrooms. Ask questions about where your child is situated when they take a nap. You don't want your child taking naps off in a corner with an obstructed view making it easier for a child to be molested. Nap times are a prime time for sexual assault on younger children.

Off-Site Trips and After-School Programs

Don't allow your child to go on any field trips unless you have full knowledge, have reviewed a consent form, and are comfortable with the parent chaperones. This happened with Mark Berndt in the Miramonte case. Berndt frequently took children on overnight field trips, which led to molestation. I would never allow my daughter to go on trips with only a male teacher. Field trips (especially overnight) present the perfect opportunity for child sexual abuse by not only teachers but students abusing other students.

Children let their guard down when they are off campus with other children and teachers. The bonding with others is multiplied since they are no longer in an artificial setting, such as a school, with strict rules. We have a case where a fifteen-year-old girl was sexually assaulted by another girl while she was sleeping. A bunch of girls had been left in a cabin without a chaperone.

Before sending a child on a field trip, parents need to do their own due diligence and ask questions. Ask about supervision, the teacher- or chaperone-to-student ratio. Ask if anyone is conducting bed checks. If so, who? Are background checks done on any volunteers?

Do not allow your child to attend an overnight field trip unless you are the chaperone or trust the chaperones attending.

Many sexual assaults occur after school, when kids and staff have their guards down and there is less supervision. The environment is more casual, and the kids are more relaxed, making it easier for molestation to occur. Talk to your child to ensure that they do not stay after school with the teacher, even for tutoring. Teachers with ill intent toward children often use tutoring as a mask for sexual intentions.

Do not allow your child to spend their lunch breaks in a classroom with a teacher, and never allow any teacher to tutor your child without your written consent. For children working with tutors, be extra vigilant when a teacher or independent adult tutor is working with your child on academics or playing a sport or musical instrument. This relationship is ripe for child sexual abuse. There are two potential land mines: First, the bonding between the child and tutor is immense and greatly accelerated due to the one-on-one time students rarely get in a standard classroom setting. The student can easily connect with the tutor on a personal level and discuss personal issues such as friendships, challenges, or issues with parents. Without the standard ethical boundaries, it can become more of a ther-apy setting. Second, many tutors share their cell numbers with the child. Don't allow that to take place. The parent should take control and clarify that all communications with the tutor to arrange appointments go through the parent. Don't let your guard down and assume an adult tutor won't do bad things to your child. Advise your child not to discuss personal issues with tutors, and let them know that they are not to exchange their own personal phone number with their tutor or to com-municate with them outside of tutoring—you will do that.

If your child is in an after-school program or day care at school, make sure to let the school know, in writing, that you do not consent to your child being released from the after-school program for any reason except into the care of a parent or guardian.

If any of these red flags are present, or if you have other rea-sons for concern, call the Childhelp National Child Abuse Hotline (1-800-4-A-Child, or 1-800-422-4453), the National Suicide Prevention Lifeline (also called the 988 Suicide and Crisis Lifeline), or 911. Please do not be afraid to escalate a concern for a child, as their well-being, and even their life, may depend on it.

TWENTY-FIVE LIFESAVING WARNINGS TO PROTECT CHILDREN

1. When something is happening to children that doesn't feel right, they don't look or seem right. Their behaviors change, patterns change, and emotional behavior can change too. If you notice a significant change in a child's appearance, personality, or habits, this may be a sign that they have or are experiencing trauma. Have they lost interest or proficiency in things they're normally excited about? Do they look unkempt or wear the same clothes all the time?

2. If there are young children at the home, are the parents' vehicles never there? If no one is in the home, ask yourself who is protecting the children.

3. Do you see a child out in the neighborhood frequently alone? Predators will notice this too, and it increases the opportunity for harm.

4. If you hear yelling and screaming coming from a home or see someone fleeing from it, especially one with children, if you aren't comfortable checking to ensure everything is okay, send the authorities to do a wellness check or call social services to check on the children. It is always better to be safe than allow children to suffer.

5. If you are aware a parent has an issue with substance abuse, an evaluation of the situation by appropriate authorities should be done to determine if there are children in the home and whether they are safe. If you're not sure who to contact, start with childcare.gov to find child protection resources in your area.

6.   If children are taking on responsibilities that are typically done by adults, that should be questioned. Buying groceries on a regular basis or young children taking care of even younger children are red flags that a parent is not present in the home.

7.   If you see a child with a tremendous amount of anger, that is a sign that something is wrong. Encourage the child to talk about what they're experiencing. If they won't talk about it, this could be a sign they need help.

8.   Check the physical layout of the campus of your child's school yourself. Be wary of classes in a detached part of the school. This can be very dangerous since there is less supervision, and it's easier to molest a child after class.

9.   When your children are younger, entering preschool, kindergarten, and even first grade, you should study the interior of classrooms. Ask questions about where your children are situated when they take a nap. You don't want your children taking naps off in a corner with an obstructed view, making it easier for a child to be molested. Nap times are a prime time for sexual assault on younger children. Younger children should be near the front of the class so that if a school administrator monitors during nap time, they can peek in the window and effectively observe. Ask whether any school administrators monitor the classes when children are napping. I would also ask that the lights be left on when children nap and blinds be left open.

10. For older children, the configuration of the classroom is also crucial. Ask your children how the classroom is arranged. We had a case in which a teacher actually put his desk behind the students instead of in front of them and molested students at their desks, since none of the other children could see it.

11. When your children are preschool, kindergarten, or elementary school age, make sure that there are working surveillance cameras installed in the classroom. Inquire about the policy of the school in preserving videotape evidence. Schools should maintain the tapes for at least thirty days.

12. Ask your child if they have been requested to be pulled out of a class by another teacher. That student could end up all alone in the other classroom with a teacher who may have ill intent.

13. Ask your child if any teachers are asking them to stay after class for extra help. A teacher spending more time than required with a student can be a red flag indicating a growing affinity that could lead to sexual abuse.

14. Ask your children if any teacher locks the door either during or after class.

15. Make sure your children do *not* accept any food or candy from any teachers. I would go one step further and provide a note to school administration that you don't consent to any teacher providing food or candy. This is a classic red flag of grooming.

16. Have your child inform you if any teacher keeps a "good child" or "bad child" list in the classroom. This signals that the teacher is going to punish the "bad children" or reward the "good children," and it could be in an improper manner or with a sexual favor. These biases should not exist in a classroom.

17. Ask your children if any teachers are taking pictures of them or if they see pictures of themselves or other students on a teacher's desk. This may be an indicator of a teacher having feelings toward a student. Provide a note to your child's school stating that you do not consent to teachers taking pictures.

18. Tell your children to share with you when a teacher writes a personal note to them and/or gives them a card. Cards and notes blur proper student-teacher boundaries and can indicate grooming. Most child sexual predators are well liked by the students. Children, and even parents, think it is cool to receive a gift from a teacher because they've been conditioned to revere teachers. While we don't want to dissuade teachers from being kind and inspiring to our children, we need to draw boundary lines on what is professional and what becomes too personal.

19. Always have your child tell you if a teacher has given them any type of gift or money.

20. Do not allow your children to spend their lunch breaks in a classroom with a teacher.

21. Many assaults take place after school. Talk to your children to ensure that they do not stay after school with the teacher, even.

22. If your children are in an after-school program or day care at school, make sure to let the school know, in writing, that you do not consent to their being released from the after-school program to go to a teacher's classroom for tutoring or to help that teacher with a project or cleaning up. There is less supervision after school by school administration.

23. Tell your children to never accept a ride from a teacher. A teacher offering a ride to a student is a classic red flag indicating perversion and a grooming process.

24. Be extra vigilant when a teacher or independent adult tutor is working with your children on academics or teaching your child to play a sport or a musical instrument. This relationship is ripe for child sexual abuse. There are some potential land mines: The bonding between the child and tutor is intense and greatly accelerated due to the one-on-one time that students rarely get in a standard classroom

setting. What can easily happen is that the student connects with the tutor on a personal level. The child starts talking about personal issues with the tutor, such as friendships, challenges, or issues at home with their parents. It can become more of a therapy setting without the standard ethical boundaries. Do not allow your child to exchange phone numbers with an adult tutor. This is a classic way for the tutor to groom a student by escalating the scholarly relationship to a personal relationship, especially via texting. The parent should take control of all communications with the tutor to arrange appointments. Make it clear to the tutor that all communications must go through the parent. Don't let your guard down and assume an adult tutor won't do bad things to your children. In addition, monitor the environment in which your children receive tutoring. For example, I won't allow my daughter to receive flute lessons unless someone else is present in the room with her and the tutor. Many times, tutoring takes place in a private, more intimate setting, which facilitates the grooming process and blurs the boundary lines for the child between what is appropriate to discuss and do and what is inappropriate. Tell your children that they should not discuss personal issues with tutors. The tutors who are child sexual predators will seize upon weaknesses in a child.

25. Don't allow your child to go on any field trips unless you have full knowledge of the trip, have reviewed a consent form, and are comfortable with the parent chaperones. Field trips (especially overnight ones) present the perfect opportunity for child sexual abuse, not only by teachers but by other students as well. Children let their guard down when they are on a trip, such as a camping expedition, with other children and teachers. The bonding with others is multiplied since children are no longer in an

artificial setting, such as school, with rigid rules. Before ever sending a child on a field trip, parents need to do their own due diligence and ask questions about supervision, including: What is the teacher- or chaperone-to-student ratio? When is bedtime? Is anyone conducting bed checks? Who? Are background checks done on all chaperones?

ABOUT THE AUTHOR

 Brian Claypool is a highly regarded trial attorney and nationally recognized legal, social, and entertainment television commentator. He is also the owner and managing general partner of the Claypool Law Firm, where he tenaciously represents and advocates for his clients. He was one of the lead attorneys in the high-profile Miramonte child sexual abuse case.

Claypool regularly contributes to Fox News, *Good Morning America*, and more.

Claypool holds a JD from Villanova University Charles Widger School of Law and a BA from Pennsylvania State University.

He is a proud single father of a precious young woman who is the light of his life. He strives to strike a balance in his life by participating in sports, political events, and various charitable organizations.